PARTIES
FOR KIDS

JUDY BASTYRA

KING*f*ISHER

NEW YORK

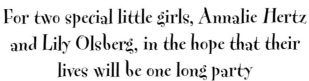

For two special little girls, Annalie Hertz and Lily Olsberg, in the hope that their lives will be one long party

KINGFISHER

Larousse Kingfisher Chambers Inc.
95 Madison Avenue
New York, New York 10016

First published in 1998
2 4 6 8 10 9 7 5 3 1

LIBRARY OF CONGRESS CATALOGING-IN-PUBLICATION DATA
Bastyra, Judy.
Parties for kids. / Judy Bastyra.—1st ed.
p. cm.
Includes index.
1. Children's parties. I. Title.
GV1205.B387   1998
793.2'1—dc21   97-31788
CIP AC

ISBN 0-7534-5092-5

Editors: Aimee Johnson, Anne Johnson, Jenny Siklós,
Eleanor Van Zandt, Belinda Weber
Designer: Sarah Goodwin
Photographers: Amanda Heywood, Ray Moller
Home economists: Carol Handslip, Netty Nicholson,
Jenny Stacey
Illustrator: Claire Chrystall

Printed in Hong Kong

Contents

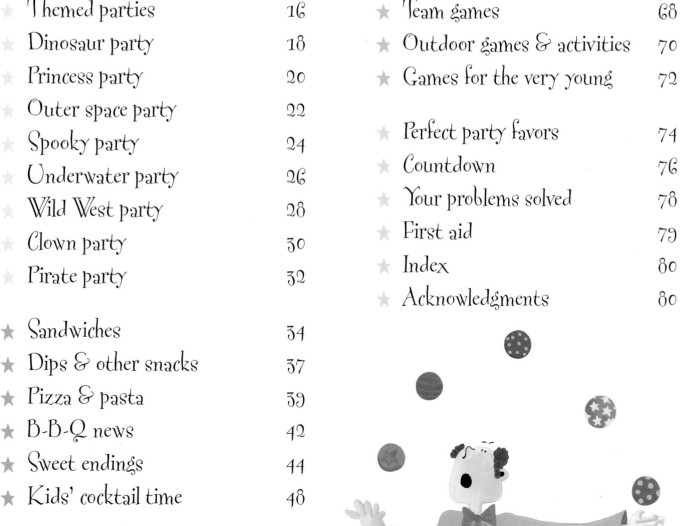

Introduction

Parties for Kids is an invaluable guide to organizing a truly memorable children's party, from the invitations to the party favors, with many ideas for theme parties, games, and delicious recipes.

A party is a special event, and you should never forget this. Children look forward to their own party for ages, and count the weeks—months even —until their special moment comes. **Parties for Kids** has been written to help take some of the stress out of giving children's parties. From the first idea to the last crumb under the chair, this book will help you give your child a party to remember.

The secret of success

The secret of success, both for a good party and for your own peace of mind, is organization. In this way, you will avoid any last-minute panic. You will also be able to look at ways of saving money, maybe by making the decorations and the party favors yourself.
Once you've set the date for the party, there are still a number of decisions you have to make. These will depend on what will suit your child, your accommodation, and your budget. The countdown at the back of the book will be especially useful to help you fit in all the preparations for the party. Here are some general points to make the party a success.

★ **Make sure everything is ready beforehand.**
★ **Be relaxed—remember this is a very special day.**
★ **Make sure you have enough helpers.**
★ **Plan more games than you need.**
★ **Make a list of who the presents are from so your child can write thank-you notes.**
★ **Have a damp cloth ready for sticky fingers.**
★ **Be prepared to deal with a mess, and have plenty of garbage bags handy.**
★ **Be specific about both the starting and ending times, and restrict the time to 2–2½ hours.**

Coping with different ages

Every child is different, of course, but these general guidelines should come in handy.

1-year-olds: These parties are as much for the parents and grandparents as for the child. One-year-olds will probably be accompanied by an adult, so include them in your plans for refreshments. The birthday child will probably be more interested in the wrapping paper than in the presents. Be prepared for tears—it can all be too much!

2-year-olds: This age group will still want a parent to stay. They are probably too young for organized games but usually enjoy dancing, so have lots of music and toys for them to play with. The party should last no longer than 1½ hours.

3-year-olds: Most three-year-olds will be happy to stay without their parents, but you should have plenty of adults to help with hugs, bathroom visits, and washing hands. They can play short games, especially ones with music.

4-year-olds: This is a magical party age, when children interact well with each other. They can become overexcited, though, so plan all the games carefully, and don't let the party go on for too long.

5-year-olds: They can be quite self-conscious at this age and may become boisterous. Plan more games than you actually need, in case they play them more quickly than you expected. Have a few calming-down games up your sleeve, in case they become too rowdy.

6-year-olds: At this age, they are starting to develop skills such as painting, gluing, and cutting, and will probably want to help you with all the preparations for the party. They have lots of energy and will want to burn some of it off—so make sure that you have plenty of room and plan some well-organized activities.

7-year-olds: At this age, children can understand the rules of games and are very cooperative, so they will enjoy some organized team games. Make sure that everyone has a chance to shine, or it may all end in tears.

8-year-olds: This is the age when many children prefer single-sex parties. Many of them also prefer to have an activity party such as swimming, bowling, or a visit to a puppet theater. This can be very expensive, so if you're paying to take them out, plan to have refreshments at home, or a picnic, to cut down on the cost.

9-year-olds: Children can be very difficult at this age because they are becoming competitive and tend to show off. Team games are excellent, as is anything that gives them a platform to perform—say, a quiz or charades, or even something more physical like a football game or sports party.

10-year-olds: Double-digits mean a leap into maturity, and ten-year-olds will want the party to be as much of a success as you do. They will help you choose the appropriate games and organize the whole event.

Invitations

Get your party off to a flying start with these jazzy invitation ideas.

Personalized invitations are a lot of fun, and these are simple to make. If you're having a themed party, set the scene right from the start with the party invitation.

Get off your horse and make this Wild West-style invitation. Push a pencil through the card to make bullet holes, then rub the edges with black crayon.

Dangle planets and moons from black thread for a 3-D space effect.

Curiosity will get the better of this cat—simply fold some stiff paper in half and cut the top of a cat's head out of the back of the card.

Pumpkin and ghost paper chains make really fantastic invitations for a spooky party.

Get the party magic working early by sending invitations on silver wands.

Dangling snakes twist and swirl in a light breeze. Cut a serpent spiral out of construction paper, and make a hole in the end to thread some string through.

Hints and tips

Keep your invitation design simple—you will need to draw it several times.

☆ **Pop-up invitations are fun to receive and are surprisingly easy to make.**

☆ **Gold or silver pens are available at most stationery stores and look striking on dark cards.**

☆ **Snakes, pigs, and sharks all make great invitations; or you could use the birthday child's favorite animal.**

X marks the spot: rub brown crayon along the torn edges of the card to make the map look older.

Flowery party pigs are a great motif for invitations. Wrap pink yarn around a pipe cleaner to make a curly tail.

Everyone's a winner with these gold medal invitations—perfect for sports parties. Cut a small hole in the top so you can thread a ribbon through.

What to do

Clowning around

You will need:
★ stiff paper
★ construction paper
★ scissors
★ thin wire
★ glue

1 Cut a piece of paper 12 x 6 inches (30 x 15cm). Fold in half. Open it out and make two 1½-inch (4cm) cuts across fold. Push through central piece of card. Make a fold so it stands up. Decorate inside of card with construction paper.

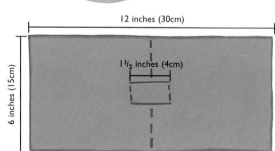

2 Cut a clown shape out of stiff paper. Your finished clown must not be taller than 5½ inches (13cm), including juggling balls. Bend thin wire above clown's head and glue it to his back. Glue three paper "balls" on the wire.

3 Glue the clown to the middle of the small piece of paper in the center, and your juggling clown is complete.

Pumpkin parade

You will need:
★ stiff orange paper, about 24 x 5½ inches (60 x 13cm)
★ yellow and orange construction paper
★ craft knife ★ glue

1 Fold stiff orange paper into a zigzag of six sections. On the front, draw your pumpkin design, making sure it goes right to the edges of the paper. Using a craft knife, cut out shape, being careful not to cut the folded edges.

2 Pull open your card, and decorate with yellow and orange construction paper. Fold the card up again, and cut out a mouth and eyes.

Shark shocker

You will need:
★ **blue, white, and gray construction paper**
★ **scissors** ★ **glue**

1 Fold a piece of gray paper in half, and draw a shark outline on it. Allow about ½ inch (1cm) at the bottom for the tabs. Add eyes, gills, and teeth.

2 Fold a piece of blue paper in half. Cut out a big water splash and several drops from the white paper. Glue these to the blue paper. Glue along the tabs.

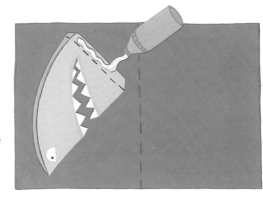

3 Place the shark in the middle of the water splash and at an angle to the center fold. Close the card and allow the glue to dry.

Dinosaur pin

You will need:
★ **stiff paper or poster board**
★ **construction paper**
★ **scissors**
★ **glue**
★ **thin rubber band**
★ **safety pin and transparent tape**

1 Fold a piece of stiff paper in half. Glue on construction paper bushes and sand. Make two small holes in the middle and thread a small piece of rubber band through. Tie the ends at the back.

2 Cut out a dinosaur shape. Attach a safety pin to the dinosaur with tape, then pin it through the loop of rubber band on front of card.

Possible venues

If the thought of hordes of overexcited kids tearing around your home fills you with dread, the answer might be to hold the party somewhere else.

If you decide to hold the party away from home, there are a few things you should take into account. If you are going any distance, you need to recruit the services (and cars!) of some of the other parents to help you with transportation. Where young children are concerned, there should always be at least one adult for every three children, to help with supervision—bathroom trips, preparing the food, or just offering a hug when necessary.

Ideas away from home

Here are some ideas for venues and parties that you can hold away from home.

Swimming pool parties: Check with your local swimming pool whether—and when—you can hold a party there. Find out if they provide a lifeguard, and if not, make sure you have enough adults coming to help you supervise the children. Try to keep all the games in the water. Children running around the edge of the pool is a recipe for disaster. Don't forget that the children are bound to have different swimming abilities, and make sure that there are some games for the less advanced swimmers—

maybe involving swimming aids such as water wings or inner tubes—as well as for the good swimmers. Some swimming pools have a special room where the children can eat, and some actually provide the food. You will have to bring the cake.

Ice-skating parties: Check with your local skating rink to see if it is possible to hold a party there. Ask if they provide instructors who will teach the children the basics of skating and make sure that they are safe on the ice. If not, make sure that there will be enough adults to supervise the children. Some skating rinks have a special room where the children can hold the party and eat after skating, and some provide the food. As with swimming parties, though, you will have to provide the cake.

Theater parties: Some children's theaters and puppet theaters are geared up for parties. The children watch the play and then they can go to a special section of the theater café to eat. Sometimes you have to prepare and bring the food yourself, or sometimes they will provide it. Either way, you will have to bring the cake.

Beach parties: If you live near a large lake, or the coast, beach parties are a good idea. You can organize lots of activities on the shore—building sand castles, making sculptures or building things out of driftwood, collecting shells, and even digging for clams. Make sure that there are enough adults to supervise the children, and don't allow them to venture off on their own.

Parties in the park: Take the children to your local park and organize plenty of different sporty games as well as some silly ones (see page 68), and create your very own "Olympics." Have lots of prizes, and try to make sure that everyone wins something.

If the weather is very hot, take plenty of drinks along, ask the children to bring sun hats (have a few to spare just in case), supply suntan lotion, and try to base yourself somewhere where there is some shade.

It may be fun to have a picnic, but make sure that most of the "Olympic" events take place before eating. If you've planned an outdoor party, it's always a good idea to have a back-up plan in case there's bad weather and the whole event is rained-out! Check out what's playing at the movie theater, or rent a video just in case.

Other party ideas

There are plenty of other parties you can hold, depending on your local facilities and what your child is interested in. Consider the following:

★ an arts and crafts party, maybe including a competition
★ a cooking party
★ a disco party
★ a camp-out-in-the-backyard party
★ a tennis party
★ a bowling party
★ soft indoor gymnasium

★ trampolining (this needs close supervision)
★ waterslide park for older children
★ rollerblading (in-line skating)
★ go-carting
★ horse riding
★ football or baseball games
★ basketball games
★ miniature golf
★ being part of an audience at a live TV show

Places of interest to visit

The idea is that the place itself will entertain the children so that you don't have to provide the entertainment. Places that make good party venues for a group of children include:

★ science museum
★ football/sports stadium
★ amusement park
★ theme park
★ zoo or farm
★ toy museum
★ car museum
★ circus
★ sports event
★ aquarium
★ theater
★ concert
★ ballet

After a couple of hours or so, you will need to feed the kids, so make sure that there is a restaurant or a picnic area and bathroom facilities nearby.

Entertainers

Many parents can't face the prospect of entertaining a group of demanding kids for two hours. That's why professional entertainers have become so popular.

Entertainers don't come cheap, but they can be invaluable for children over the age of three or four. If you choose the right one, you are guaranteed a successful party.

Finding an entertainer

The best way of finding an entertainer is by word of mouth—preferably from another parent who has recently thrown a successful party. But this is not always possible.

Other ways are to look at advertisements in your local newspaper or telephone directory, but this is probably the least reliable method of all because there's no way of knowing how good someone is. If you call someone cold, ask for a recommendation from someone for whom they have worked recently.

If the entertainers operate under a character name, such as "Tommy the Clown" or "Twinkle Toes," they may be part of an organization that uses many different people dressed up as the same character and some may be better than others. It is therefore well worth finding out who is the best and making sure you get that one.

Asking the right questions

Different entertainers provide different services, and it is always a good idea to find out exactly what they will provide for the money.

★ **Do they provide just the entertainment, or do they also organize games?**
★ **Is their show suitable for your child's age?**
★ **Do they give prizes? If so, what kind and how many? Will every child receive one?**
★ **Do they give party favors?**
★ **Do they help with the food?**
★ **How long do they stay?**
★ **Do they have a helper?**

Which entertainer?

There is a whole host of entertainers to choose from. You know your child and will be aware of what would suit him or her. Your best bet is to choose an entertainer who doesn't concentrate too much on any one thing, so that the children don't get bored.

Magicians: They will provide a show of magic tricks. Some of them make balloon animals for the children to take home—make sure that they make one for each child—and the highlight may be a live rabbit which all the children can pet.

Sports organizers: Some sports clubs have qualified instructors who will organize a children's sports party. There are as many different types of sports party as there are sports, such as football, baseball, swimming, tennis, and gymnastics.

Clowns: These come in many guises, but most of them just make the children laugh. Some of them perform magic tricks, and others also organize games.

Face painters: This is a very popular form of entertainment. Imagine being able to transform yourself into a monster, a cat, or an alien! The only drawback is that each child has to wait their turn.

Puppeteers: These come in all shapes and sizes, from hand puppets to marionettes. A clever puppeteer will involve the children in the show, but you cannot expect the children to sit still for too long, so ask if they organize games, too.

Jugglers: A juggler will not keep the attention of children for very long unless he is also teaching them the skill. This is most suitable for older children, and the juggler can also organize some games.

Craft projects: There are many enthusiastic arts and crafts teachers who enjoy spending an hour or two over the weekend taking a group project. Make sure each child makes something to take home.

Storytellers: These appeal to more imaginative children. Storytelling parties work best for a maximum of eight children.

Dance teachers: If your child is crazy about dance, a dance party is just the thing for you. Ask your local dance school if they have a teacher who will organize a party.

Animal trainers: They will bring a collection of animals to the party and introduce them to the children. Some have cats, rabbits, guinea pigs, and so on, while some have more exotic animals such as tarantulas and snakes.

Advance booking

Good entertainers need to be booked in advance, so call as soon as possible. Write to them to confirm exactly what they have agreed to provide, and include the following information:

★ **the date and time of the party**
★ **the age of the child**
★ **the number of children**
★ **the address of the party**
★ **how long the party will be**

Call a few days later to make sure that they have received the details. Call again, two or three days before the party, to make sure that the entertainer is definitely going to turn up. This sounds time-consuming but it is well worth it. It is a good idea to have an alternative plan ready, even if you do hire an entertainer, as they may canel due to a sudden illness or some other problem. Be prepared and check out the local movie theater in advance or rent a video—just in case of disaster.

Setting the scene

Parties are all about celebrating, which is why it is so important to set the scene. This says "party" instantly and gets everyone in the mood, right from the start.

There are several ways of setting the scene, the most important one being decorations. These can either be bought ready-made or, if you're feeling creative, they can be homemade.

Buying decorations

There are lots of decorations on the market that can create an instant party atmosphere. These include balloons, streamers, banners, themed paper tablecloths, paper plates and cups, party hats, horns, and so on.

The best place to get these is one of the many specialist party stores around, which are now becoming increasingly common. They are well worth a visit anyway, if only to get some inspirational ideas.

If you don't have a specialist party store near you, many of these items can be bought at a local toy or stationery store. The streamers and banners can be kept in a special box and used each time you have a party.

You can blow up balloons yourself, or you can buy special hand-held pumps. These are inexpensive and easy to use—even by the children themselves. Some party stores have heavy-duty pumps, which are even easier and more efficient to use, and they may rent one to you for a nominal charge if you buy your balloons from them.

Most party stores will fill balloons with helium for you. If you are using the balloons outside, however, make sure to secure them firmly, otherwise they will float away, never to be seen again. However you've filled them, balloons should then be grouped in bunches and tied. It's a good idea to tie them to the mailbox or the front door to help guests find your party.

Many people hold their parties in a school or social hall. This way, they don't have to worry

Can I help?

Kids enjoy all the party preparations, such as blowing up balloons.

about the mess, the noise, or the space. But these places usually need livening up with some decorations, so take some with you and brighten up the space a few hours before the party begins.

Homemade decorations

Your child will love it if you make some of the decorations yourself—proud cries of "Mommy made those" might even be heard. This may be the first party you've given for your child, but it won't be the last (not if it's the great success that it's bound to be!). There are lots of useful items for making your own decorations, which you can keep handy in a box for when the occasion arises. Useful things to have available include:

- ★ corrugated cardboard
- ★ cardboard boxes
- ★ old newspapers
- ★ old sheets/fabric remnants
- ★ colored string
- ★ ribbons
- ★ tinsel
- ★ paints
- ★ colored markers
- ★ glue and glitter glue
- ★ transparent tape
- ★ scissors
- ★ craft knife
- ★ stapler

Things to make

It may be worth spending some time making a few decorations that you can use again and again. If you're giving a birthday party, for example, you can make a birthday banner with the child's name and age, or just "Happy Birthday," then it can be used for anyone in the family. A Mexican piñata (see page 75) is a great idea. It provides great excitement and fun for the children, and a wonderful finale to the party.

Music

Lastly, don't forget that music is important in making any party fun and lively. Each age group has its favorite tunes, from nursery rhymes for the very young to the latest hit records for older children. A portable CD player will come in handy and you could put on your own favorite music while you are preparing for the party, just to get yourself in the mood.

Themed parties

If you're stuck for ideas, a themed party may be the answer. It's not only a lot of fun, it also gives you a framework within which to plan those all-important details—the costumes, the food, and even the games.

If this is the first themed party that you've thrown for your child, it may be worth spending some time making the costumes yourself from things in your closets or garage. You will be able to use them again and again for future parties. There are a lot of things you probably have already lying around the house that will come in handy for costume making and dressing up.

These include the following:

★ leotards ★ leggings
★ T-shirts, long- and short-sleeved
★ turtle-necked sweaters and T-shirts
★ paper towel tubes
★ corrugated cardboard
★ garbage bags
★ bubble wrap
★ toilet paper tubes
★ cotton balls
★ knitting yarn
★ adhesive-backed Velcro
★ scraps of fabric
★ pieces of net
★ old sheets
★ old clothes
★ rubber boots
★ tennis shoes
★ felt
★ old jeans
★ glue
★ transparent tape
★ double-sided tape
★ glitter glue
★ mesh fruit bags
★ tissue paper
★ adhesive for gluing felt
★ cardboard

Making the costumes

Costumes can be bought or rented from specialist party or costume stores, but that's an easy way out. If you have the time and energy, it is a lot more satisfying to make something yourself. Your child is bound to appreciate your efforts, and as a result, your child's costume will look completely different from everyone else's. All the costumes that we've created for this book look great—we hope you agree. But don't worry—they're not difficult. They are all, in fact, surprisingly easy to make and require no special dressmaking

Measuring your child

This illustration shows you how to take your child's measurements.

1 **Height**
Measure from the top of the head to the floor without shoes.

2 **Chest**
Place the tape measure around the body so it is positioned across the chest and over the shoulder blades.

3 **Waist**
Measure around the natural waistline.

4 **Inside leg**
Place the tape measure at the very top of the inside leg and measure to the desired length.

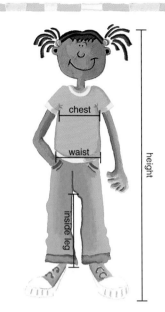

skills or fancy equipment.

The instructions are all straightforward and very simple to follow. You can use your own imagination and incorporate whatever fabrics and accessories that you have on hand in order to add your own special, personal touch.

All of the patterns that are given here should fit children between about five and nine. In the box above, we tell you how to measure your own child to adapt the pattern to his or her age and size.

All the patterns are shown in miniature. Use large sheets of brown wrapping paper and drawing aids, such as a ruler and compass, to draw the full-size pattern pieces. Just be sure to follow the measurements that are given on the diagrams.

The best clothes to wear under any costumes are matching-color T-shirts or turtlenecks, and leggings (tights will be too slippery unless the child also wears shoes).

Dinosaur party

Dinosaurs are a big favorite with all children.
To create the right atmosphere, turn the room into
a primeval rain forest with giant palm trees
and ferns.

This friendly
dinosaur is not
one of the man-
eating species.

Cave people
keep warm and
snug in furs.

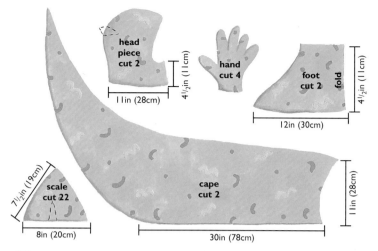

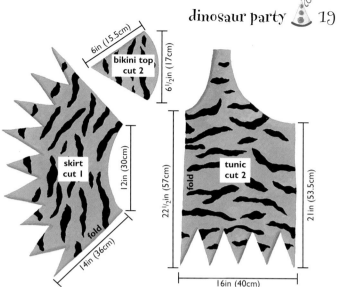

Dinosaur costume

You will need:

★ 1 ³/₄ yards (1.5m) yellow felt, 1 ³/₄ yards (1.5m) wide

★ adhesive-backed Velcro

★ orange, brown, purple, and green fabric paints

1 Draw the pattern to scale and cut out the fabric. Draw around your child's hand, and cut out. Paint each piece and leave to dry for at least three hours.

2 Sew all the darts on the headpiece and on the scales.

3 Pin half the scales, right sides together, onto one side of the head and cape pieces. Make sure the scales are pointing downward. Then pin on the other side of the head and cape pieces, right sides together (sandwiching the scales in between them). Sew together and turn right-side out.

4 Gather the cape around the neck and sew to the headpiece. Attach adhesive-backed Velcro to the neck to fasten. Sew the feet along the front seam. Sew around the outline of the hand pieces, and slip on like a glove.

Cave people's costumes

For each costume you will need:

★ 1 ¹/₈ yards (1m) fake fur

★ elastic for waistband

★ black woven tape/ribbon

★ scraps of fake fur for arm and leg bands

1 Cut out the fabric for the cave people's costumes, following the pattern.

2 Sew together the side and shoulders of the caveman's tunic.

3 Sew the side seam of the cavewoman's skirt. Then pin and sew a tape/ribbon casing around the waist. Insert some elastic to fit the size of your child's waist, and tie the ends together in a knot.

4 For the girl's bikini top, sew the two cups together in the middle, then attach tape to the cups to fit around the neck and around the back.

5 Cut the fake fur scraps into 2-inch (5cm) wide strips and use these to decorate the arms and legs, and to tie the hair.

Princess party

Little girls are guaranteed to love these costumes so much that they'll use them again and again—not just for parties but for dressing-up games at home, too.

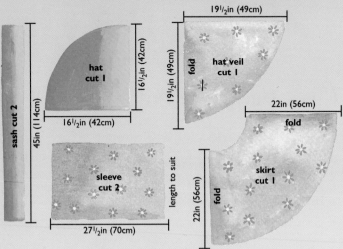

sash cut 2
45in (114cm)

hat cut 1
16½in (42cm)
16½in (42cm)

hat veil cut 1
fold
19½in (49cm)
19½in (49cm)

fold
22in (56cm)

skirt cut 1
fold
22in (56cm)

sleeve cut 2
27½in (70cm)
length to suit

For each costume

You will need:
- ★ 1 leotard
- ★ 2¼ yards (2m) chiffon (or marquisette), 1¾ yards (1.5m) wide
- ★ 1⅛ yards (1m) bias binding
- ★ elastic
- ★ gold or silver ribbon
- ★ cardboard
- ★ glue
- ★ 1⅛ yards (1m) silver fabric, 1¼ yards (1.2m) wide

1 Draw pattern to scale and cut out sleeves, hat veil, and skirt (in a full circle). Hem with zigzag stitch. Sew casing around waist, leaving a gap. Cut elastic to fit waist, thread through, and knot.

2 Zigzag stitch around the edge of the sleeves and gather around the top of them. Then pin the sleeves to the shoulders or sleeves of the leotard, and sew these in place.

3 Stitch the sash together with a center seam. Then hem around the edges by hand.

4 Cut out hat from cardboard and cover in fabric. Then glue together the back edges of the hat. Hem around the edges of the hat veil, and then sew to the top of the hat. Sew elastic to the hat to fit under the chin.

Princesses

Fairytales and films have encouraged lots of little girls to dream of being a beautiful fairy princess. Indulge their dreams by helping them dress the part—they'll look terrific!

Nothing makes a little girl
feel more elegant than
a tall hat.

Outer space party

This is the ideal theme for a group of imaginative eight-year-old children. The birthday child can be the captain of the spaceship, in charge of the control panel.

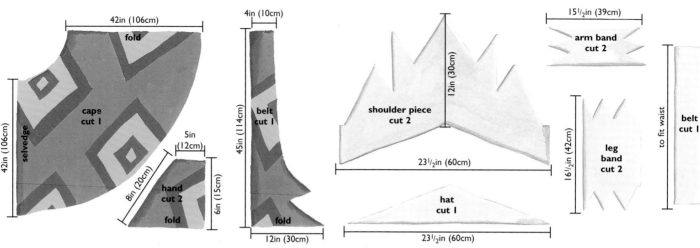

Alien costume

You will need:
★ 48 x 80 inches (1.2 x 2m) bubble wrap
★ acrylic paint for bubble wrap
★ acrylic spray paint for headpiece
★ adhesive-backed Velcro
★ inexpensive basketball for headpiece
★ face paint

1 Draw the pattern to scale and cut out the bubble wrap for the cloak, gloves, and belt. Decorate with paint and make a fastening around the neck with the adhesive-backed Velcro.

2 Cut the basketball in half, spray with paint and allow to dry. When you have applied face paint, put on the headpiece.

Spaceman costume

You will need:
★ 4 large sheets of silver poster board
★ adhesive-backed Velcro
★ fluorescent tape, for decoration

1 Cut out all the shapes for the spaceman from the silver poster board, following the pattern, and assemble the pieces using the Velcro.

2 Decorate this intergalactic costume with well-positioned strips of fluorescent tape, as shown in the picture.

No space trip would be complete without an amazing alien.

Turtlenecks, leggings and spray-on glitter make these out-of-this-world costumes complete.

Spooky party

Kids just love dressing up as ghoulish ghosts. To create the right atmosphere, spray cobwebs on the windows and hang spiders from the ceiling.

Witch costume

You will need:

★ 2¼ yards (2m) net
★ elastic
★ 2¼ yards (2m) green ribbon
★ 2 strong black garbage bags
★ 2 pieces of black poster board
★ glitter paint
★ mesh fruit bag
★ 1 large green garbage bag

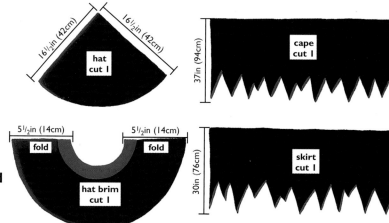

hat cut 1 — 16½in (42cm), 16½in (42cm)

cape cut 1 — 37in (94cm)

petticoat cut 1

5½in (14cm) fold — hat brim cut 1 — 5½in (14cm) fold

skirt cut 1 — 30in (76cm)

1 Cut the net to twice the length of your child for the petticoat. Fold in half lengthwise and make a casing along the fold. Thread elastic through the casing and tie into a knot.

2 Open the top of the black plastic bag and pull into a cylinder shape to make a skirt. Cut the hem into zigzags and cut holes 2 inches (5cm) from the top, and 3 inches (7cm) apart. Thread ribbon through the holes. For the cape: cut along top and sides of the second bag, and open it out flat. Cut holes about 2 inches (5cm) from the top and 3 inches (7cm) apart. Thread ribbon through holes and tie into a cape.

3 Cut out hat and brim from black poster board and decorate. Glue back edges of hat together and attach brim, snipping inside sections at intervals. For wig: cut green bag into 1-inch (2.5cm) strips and pull a strip through each hole in the mesh bag, and knot in the middle. Thread elastic through the outer holes in mesh fruit bag and knot in the middle.

Ghost costume

You will need:

★ 1 old, white sheet
★ black felt, cut into 3½-inch (8cm) circles
★ fabric glue

1 Place the sheet over your child's head and mark the position of the eyes on the outside of it.

2 Glue the black felt circles in place, then cut out the centers, making two peep holes.

Mummy

You will need:
- ★ **3 rolls of white toilet paper**
- ★ **masking tape**

Wrap the child loosely in white toilet paper. Before you start winding it around them, make sure their limbs are slightly bent or they will find it difficult to walk. Secure the paper with masking tape.

Few people would like to meet this witch on a dark night!

Underwater party

Transform the room into a giant aquarium with tinsel, streamers, strips of cellophane, and shells. Hang tropical fish and jellyfish from the ceiling.

Every little girl will jump at the chance to be a mermaid— with legs!

A scuba diver wears black, a swimming mask, snorkel, and flippers. Make the air tanks with two large plastic bottles sprayed blue.

The King of the Sea looks suitably royal!

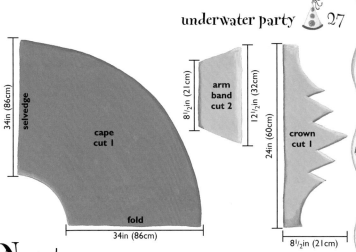

Mermaid

You will need:

- ★ 1¹/₈ yards (1m) green felt, 1³/₄ yards (1.5m) wide
- ★ 10 inches (25cm) of felt in each of three colors for scales
- ★ 2¹/₄ yards (2m)
- gold braid to assemble bikini
- ★ fabric glue
- ★ gold glitter glue
- ★ 2 plastic bags
- ★ mesh fruit bag, for wig
- ★ elastic

1 Draw pattern and cut out tail, bikini top, and as many scales as you want. Glue scales onto tail, starting from the bottom and grading colors as you go. Keep some scales to cover the side seams.

2 Sew the side seams of the tail, leaving an opening for the casing. Make the waist casing and thread elastic through to fit your child's waist. Knot the ends.

3 Sew a double seam to reinforce tail, and glue on the remaining scales to cover side seams. Decorate tail with glitter glue. Make the top as for cavewoman on page 19. Decorate with glitter glue.

4 To make wig, cut plastic bags into 1-inch (2.5cm) strips. Thread elastic through holes in mesh bag. Pull plastic strips through and knot in center.

Neptune

You will need:

- ★ 2¹/₄ yards (2m) dark green lining fabric, wide enough to fit child's height from shoulder to floor
- ★ 1¹/₈ yards (1m) each green, turquoise, and yellow net
- ★ adhesive-backed Velcro
- ★ gold poster board
- ★ stapler
- ★ 1¹/₈ yards (1m) gold braid
- ★ 2 white plastic bags
- ★ mesh fruit bag for wig
- ★ elastic
- ★ beard

1 Draw the pattern to scale, and cut out the cape and the strips of green, turquoise, and yellow net. Hem the front edges of the cape and around the bottom edge, and gather neck.

2 Sew on the strips of net to look like pieces of seaweed, and make a fastening around the neck with the adhesive-backed Velcro.

3 Cut out Neptune's crown, following the pattern. Staple the back edges together to fit your child's head.

4 Make the wig using the white plastic bags and following the instructions for the mermaid's wig, left.

Wild West party

This is the perfect theme for boisterous boys aged about eight or nine, who are bound to enjoy dressing up as rough and rugged cowboys.

This is the age at which children enjoy slumber parties. Don't invite too many kids or they'll never get any sleep!

Slumber party

Six is a good limit for a slumber party—more than that and they won't sleep. Invite them with their sleeping bags and preferably not before about 4 or 5p.m. Summer is the best time of year for this kind of theme, as you can combine it with a barbecue, after some games. A cowboy video is a good way for the children to wind down before they go to bed.

Dressing up as cowboys (and cowgirls) is easy.

Cowboy hats and sheriff badges complete the picture.

Cowboys

Cowboys do not need any special outfits, so this is one of the easiest costumes of all, requiring very minimal work—just a little (inexpensive) shopping. All young cowboys need is some jeans, a plaid shirt, a bandanna, and some fake stubble with face paint. Cowboy hats are readily available from costume and party stores.

Playing with the cowboys

A good thing to do at a Wild West party is to have a scavenger hunt. Go in pairs or small groups, each of which is given a bag to carry their booty. For older children, give them a list of things to find and tell them the limits of the area for their search. Give them a time limit to find the objects, and blow a whistle or ring a bell when time is up. Some ideas might include:

★ a dropped candy wrapper
★ a forked twig
★ 3 white stones
★ 5 blades of grass
★ a feather
★ an acorn
★ a leaf

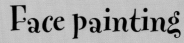

Face painting

Dressing up as cowboys is a good opportunity for some imaginative face painting, with mustaches, beards, scars, and stubble being strong favorites.

Clown party

A clown party is a great theme for young children between the ages of four and seven. Hire a clown entertainer or some face paint artists.

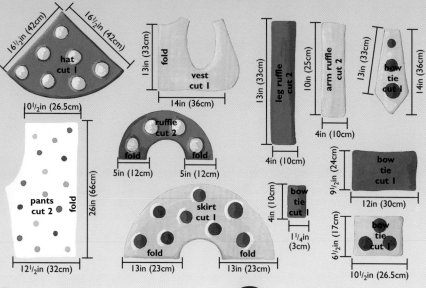

hat
cut 1

16½in (42cm)   16½in (42cm)

10½in (26.5cm)

pants
cut 2   fold

26in (66cm)

12½in (32cm)

vest
cut 1   fold

13in (33cm)

14in (36cm)

ruffle
cut 2

fold   fold

5in (12cm)   5in (12cm)

skirt
cut 1

fold   fold

13in (23cm)   13in (23cm)

leg ruffle
cut 2

13in (33cm)

4in (10cm)

arm ruffle
cut 2

10in (25cm)

4in (10cm)

bow
tie
cut 1

13in (33cm)   14in (36cm)

bow
tie
cut 1

4in (10cm)

1¼in (3cm)

bow
tie
cut 1

6½in (17cm)

bow
tie
cut 1

9½in (24cm)

12in (30cm)

10½in (26.5cm)

Boy clown

You will need:

★ 1⅛ yards (1m) fabric for pants, 1¾ yards (1.5m) wide
★ 1⅛ yards (1m) felt, 1¾ yards (1.5m) wide for the vest, bow tie, and ruffles
★ 12 x 12 inches (30 x 30cm) red felt for spots on bow tie
★ 2 large buttons
★ 1⅛ yards (1m) red rickrack
★ elastic
★ 2 pom-poms made from rainbow-colored yarn
★ adhesive-backed Velcro

1 Draw pattern to scale and cut out all the pieces. With right sides facing, sew the pants around the crotch and along the inside legs. Make a casing around the waist and ankles, and thread with elastic. Sew on trimming for vest, stitch up shoulder seams and sew on two giant buttons.

2 Decorate yellow bow tie with red dots. Thread both bows through the blue casing, overcast in place, and sew on yellow bow tie. Sew bias binding as a casing in the center of ruffles, thread with elastic, and tie off.

Girl clown

You will need:
★ 1 1/8 yards (1m) felt,
   1 3/4 yards (1.5m) wide for skirt
★ 30 inches (75cm) felt for ruffles
★ scraps of felt for dots
★ 1 1/8 yards (1m) yellow net, for petticoat
★ 3 3/8 yards (3m) elastic
★ 1 3/4 yards (1.5m) yellow bias binding
★ 1 pom-pom made from rainbow-colored yarn
★ fabric glue

1 Draw pattern, to scale, and cut out the skirt, petticoat, ruffles, and dots (using scraps).

2 Make skirt and neck ruffle by sewing a casing, inserting elastic, and tying off. Decorate with colored dots.

3 Make petticoat by sewing a casing along fold and inserting elastic. Sew ends together.

4 Make leg/hand ruffles by sewing bias binding and inserting elastic. Sew pom-pom on T-shirt.

Clowning around comes naturally to most kids.

Attach Velcro to back of pom-poms and glue on top of the shoes.

Clown hats

You will need:
★ 1 large sheet of poster board
★ 20 inches (50cm) each yellow and blue felt
★ scraps of red felt
★ fabric glue
★ 1 ball of rainbow-colored yarn for the hair
★ 2 pom-poms made from rainbow-colored yarn

1 Cut out the hats from poster board, following the pattern, and cover with felt. Then cut out 16-inch (40cm) lengths of yarn and gather into bundles of eight. Sew to edge of hat and trim.

2 Sew pom-pom to hat and decorate with dots. Staple edges of hat to form a cone.

Pirate party

Hoist the sails and pull up the gangplank—this is strictly for bold children, as these fearless pirates venture into murky, shark-infested waters.

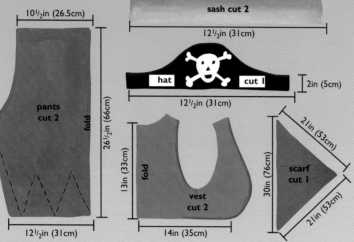

Pirate costume

You will need:

★ 1 1/8 yards (1m) cotton fabric, 1 1/4 yards (1.2m) wide, for pants
★ 1 1/8 yards (1m) felt, 1 3/4 yards (1.5m) wide, for vest
★ 1 3/4 yards (1.5m) braid
★ 4 buttons
★ 30 inches (75cm) cotton fabric, for sash and scarf
★ black and white poster board
★ fabric glue
★ elastic
★ silver poster board for buckles
★ adhesive-backed Velcro

1 Draw pattern to scale, cut out pieces, and make pants following clown instructions on page 30.

Shiver me timbers! Pirates rule the sea at partytime.

2 Sew the shoulder seams of the vest together. Hand-sew the braid around the edge and sew on the buttons.

3 Hem the edges of the scarf and the sash. Cut out the hat from the black poster board, and skull and crossbones from the white poster board– then glue them to the hat. Measure the child's head, and use Velcro to fasten the hat at the back.

4 Make buckles out of silver poster board and attach them to shoes with the Velcro.

Aargh, Jim lad... me hearties!

Buccaneer costume

You will need:
★ 1 1/8 yards (1m) felt, 1 3/4 yards (1.5m) wide
★ elastic

1 Draw the pattern to scale and cut out the pants. Cut zigzags around the bottoms of both pant legs.

2 Sew around crotch and inside legs. Then make a casing around the waist and thread elastic through. Make hat, sash, scarf, and shoe buckles as for the pirate.

Land ahoy!

Skull and crossbones, eye patches, mustaches, and blacked-out teeth... all designed to make these nice little boys look as fierce as can be!

Sandwiches

Celebration sandwiches should be special.
They can be made from different kinds of bread and
filled with a variety of fillings, including sweet ones.
Use your imagination to create your own combinations.

Sandwich secrets

☆ **Make sandwiches with bread that is one day old, as it will be firmer.**

☆ **Chill a loaf of white bread before you slice it.**

☆ **A hot knife makes it easier to cut bread.**

☆ **Keep sandwiches fresh by placing them in plastic bags or covering them with a clean, damp cloth.**

☆ **Take margarine or butter out of the fridge to soften a couple of hours before you begin.**

☆ **Use different types of bread to add variety to your party sandwiches. Choose from rye, wholewheat, French bread, ciabatta, chollah, pita, rolls or buns, and English muffins.**

Pinwheels

Makes 36–42
You will need:
★ **1 unsliced brown or white loaf of bread, preferably sandwich-type**
★ **butter or margarine, softened**
★ **chosen filling**

Cut bread into thin slices lengthwise and remove the crusts. Spread with butter or margarine and then add the filling. Roll up each slice of bread and secure with foil or plastic wrap. Chill for an hour before cutting into slices.

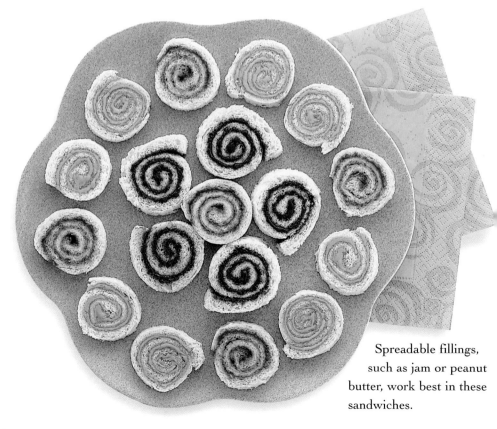

Spreadable fillings, such as jam or peanut butter, work best in these sandwiches.

Chocolate bagels

Serves 5
You will need:
* ★ 5 bagels
* ★ 8 oz. (250g) melted chocolate
* ★ slices of fruit, such as banana, strawberry, and pineapple

Slice the bagels in half and remove all the doughy white

inside from the bottom halves. Fill with melted chocolate, and add the fruit before it sets. Add the top half, and heat in the oven until the bagels are crisp.

Warn children to be careful when they bite into the bagels, as the melted chocolate will be hot.

Egg salad

Makes 4–5 sandwiches
You will need:
* ★ 4 hard-boiled eggs
* ★ 2 tablespoons mayonnaise
* ★ salt and pepper
* ★ 1 tablespoon mustard

Rinse the hot hard-boiled eggs under cold water to prevent the yolks from turning black. Peel and chop or mash the eggs with a fork. Add the mayonnaise and mustard and mix well. Season to taste.

Eggspress train

Allow 1–2 sandwiches per child
You will need:
* ★ brown and white sliced bread
* ★ butter, softened
* ★ egg salad filling
* ★ other chosen fillings
* ★ carrots, celery, bell peppers, tomatoes, and pretzel sticks

Butter the bread and make it into sandwiches with fillings of your choice. Cut into freight car-shaped rectangles and make a locomotive. Push slices of carrot onto toothpicks for wheels. Balance the sandwiches on the sticks and decorate.

Slices of celery, green, yellow, and red bell peppers, sweet cherry tomatoes, and pretzel sticks make delicious edible cargo.

If you have problems balancing the sandwiches on the toothpicks, cut a piece of cardboard and put the sandwich on this.

Add the finishing touch to the train by cutting a wisp of smoke from an extra slice of white bread.

Monster rolls

Makes 10 rolls
You will need:

★ 10 different-shaped rolls
★ butter or margarine, softened
★ ham, bologna, salami, and cheese for fillings
★ salad ingredients for decoration
★ wooden toothpicks

Cut each roll halfway across to make a mouth, and spread the inside with butter or margarine. Cut the meat into tongue shapes and the cheese into teeth shapes.

Arrange the meat and cheese inside the rolls. Decorate with eyes, noses, ears, and hair, securing them with the toothpicks (remember to remove these before eating!).

Sticks of cheese look great as hair!

Open-faced sandwiches

Makes 4 sandwiches
You will need:

★ 4 slices of brown or white bread
★ various toppings, such as cream and cottage cheese, chocolate spread, fruit, vegetables, salami, eggs, and candies

Spread a different topping on each slice of bread. Decorate each topping with appropriate garnishes, making faces, boats, or flowers.

Grapes, banana, and strawberries taste wonderful with chocolate spread.

Make eyes out of radishes with thin slices of olive on top.

Sail away on a sea of cottage cheese in a pepper boat.

Can I help?

Encourage your child's creativity by getting her to design the pictures for the sandwiches.

Dips & other snacks

The secret of a successfully balanced party menu is to have a variety of colorful snacks that look as appealing as the sweet treats.

Things to dip

Carrot sticks, celery, tortilla chips, broccoli, cherry tomatoes, and potato chips.

Spinach dip

Serves 8
You will need:
- ★ 6 oz. (175g) frozen spinach, defrosted
- ★ ⅝ cup (150ml) sour cream
- ★ 2 tablespoons mayonnaise
- ★ salt and pepper

Drain the spinach in a strainer and pat dry with paper towels. Put all the ingredients in a food processor and blend together.

Cream cheese dip

Serves 8
You will need:
- ★ 8 oz. (230g) cream cheese
- ★ ⅝ cup (150ml) sour cream
- ★ 2 tablespoons chopped chives
- ★ salt and pepper

Put all the ingredients in a food processor and blend together.

Cheese crackers

Makes about 25 crackers
You will need:
- ★ ½ cup (115g) margarine
- ★ 2 cups (230g) all-purpose flour
- ★ pinch of salt
- ★ 2 egg yolks
- ★ ½ cup (55g) grated Cheddar cheese
- ★ 2 tablespoons ketchup
- ★ 1 egg, beaten

Preheat the oven to 400°F (200°C). Mix the margarine, flour, and salt together in a bowl until it resembles breadcrumbs. Stir in the egg yolks, grated cheese, and ketchup. Mix together and form into a ball. Roll out the dough on a floured surface until it is about ¼ inch (5mm) thick, and cut into shapes. Transfer the dough shapes to a greased baking sheet and brush the tops with the beaten egg. Bake for 12 minutes, then transfer to a rack to cool.

Cheese dinosaur

Serves 8–10
You will need:
★ 1 pineapple
★ 1 kiwi fruit
★ 2 raisins
★ 8oz. (230g) hard cheese,
  such as Cheddar, Monterey Jack, or Gouda

Cut a large slice from the top of the pineapple, and remove some of the leaves. Cut the legs shape from the bottom of the fruit and scoop out the flesh (set aside to use later). Cut the cheese into triangles of various sizes. Cut the pineapple flesh into ½-inch 1cm) cubes. Insert toothpicks into the outside of the dinosaur, and use them to secure first the pineapple pieces, then the cheese triangles. To make the head, peel the kiwi fruit and cut out a slice for the mouth. Attach the raisin eyes with toothpicks, and use a pineapple leaf as a tongue. Attach the head to the body by pushing another toothpick through the center of the crown of the pineapple.

Tomato and tuna owlets

Makes 12 owlets
You will need:
★ 12 small tomatoes
★ small can of tuna fish in water, drained
★ 1 hard-boiled egg
★ 2 tablespoons mayonnaise
★ 2 teaspoons ketchup
★ several stuffed green olives, cut into slices
★ lettuce, to serve

Halve the tomatoes and scoop out the seeds. Using a fork, mash together the tuna fish, egg, mayonnaise, and ketchup in a bowl. Pile the mixture into half of the cut tomatoes. Cut any remaining tomato halves into triangles for the beaks and ears. Decorate the filled tomato halves with the beaks and ears, then add the olive eyes. Serve on a nest of roughly-torn lettuce.

Pizza and pasta

Create your own Little Italy with loads of pasta and pizza. Nothing makes kids happier, or fills them up faster!

Pizza dough

Makes 2 8-inch (20cm) pizzas
You will need:
★ 2¹/₂ cups (285g) all-purpose flour
★ I teaspoon salt
★ I envelope dried yeast
★ 2 tablespoons olive oil
★ I cup (230ml) hot water

Sift together the flour and salt, then add the yeast, oil, and hot water, and mix into a dough. On a floured work surface, knead the dough for 5 minutes until it is shiny and elastic. Put the dough into a clean bowl, cover it, and leave it to rise in a warm place for 1 hour.

Tomato sauce

Makes 2 8-inch (20cm) pizzas
You will need:
★ 2 tablespoons olive oil
★ I small onion, chopped
★ 2 tablespoons tomato paste
★ 16-oz. (450g) can chopped
 tomatoes, drained
★ I teaspoon dried oregano
★ ¹/₂ teaspoon salt
★ ¹/₂ teaspoon sugar
★ pinch of ground black pepper
★ mushrooms, olives, and green
 bell pepper, to decorate

Heat the oil in a saucepan, add the onion, and cook gently for 5 minutes. Add the tomato paste, chopped tomatoes (drained first), and oregano, and season well. Cook for 15 minutes more. Allow to cool.

Pizza snake

Serves 8–10 children
You will need:
★ flour for rolling out dough
★ 2 tablespoons olive oil
★ I quantity of pizza dough
★ I quantity of tomato sauce
★ mozzarella cheese, sliced
★ 2 mushrooms, sliced
★ black olives
★ green bell pepper, for tongue

Preheat the oven to 350°F (180°C). Roll the pizza dough into a sausage shape. Lay it in a spiral on a lightly oiled baking sheet, and flatten to form the snake's body. Spread with tomato sauce, then add a row of mozzarella. Decorate the cheese with mushrooms and olives. Brush with olive oil and bake in the top of the oven for 15–20 minutes. Add olive rings for the eyes and make a tongue with the green bell pepper.

Give your snake a pair of beady eyes with black olive rings, and a tasty tongue with a piece of green bell pepper.

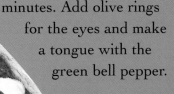

Express pizzas

If you don't have time to make your own pizza dough, just buy ready-made crusts from the supermarket and create your own designs.

Heavenly pizzas

Makes 2 mini-pizzas
You will need:
★ I tablespoon olive oil
★ 2 small pizza crusts
★ I quantity tomato sauce
★ 2 cheese slices
★ 3 thick mozzarella slices
To decorate:
★ black and green olives
★ slices of red bell pepper

Heat the oven to 350°F (180°C) and brush a baking sheet with oil. Cut out a star shape from one of the crusts, using kitchen scissors. Cut out star shapes from the cheese slices and the rocket designs from the mozzarella cheese. Brush both pizza crusts with oil, and cover with tomato sauce. Bake for 8 minutes. Remove from the oven and cover the star with the cheese slice stars and the whole pizza with the rocket and star shapes. Decorate the pizzas with olives, then bake for another 5 minutes.

Pizza tiger

Serves 4–6
You will need:
★ I tablespoon olive oil
★ 2 medium pizza crusts
★ I quantity of tomato sauce
★ 8 oz. (230g) American Cheddar cheese
★ 8 oz. (230g) mozzarella cheese
★ 2 stuffed green olives, for eyes
★ fresh chives, for whiskers

Heat the oven to 350°F (180°C). Brush a large baking sheet with oil. Cut a tiger's head and tail from one of the crusts, and a small piece from the top of the other crust, where the head will fit. Assemble the tiger on the baking sheet, brush with oil, and cover with tomato sauce. Make the nose, ears, and stripes out of cheese. Cook for 15–20 minutes, then remove from the oven and add the olive eyes and chive whiskers.

A pizza tiger looks as friendly as he is tasty.

Tomato sauce for pasta

Serves 4–6

You will need:

★ 2 tablespoons olive oil
★ 1 large onion, peeled and finely chopped
★ 2 garlic cloves, crushed
★ 2 16-oz. (450g) cans chopped tomatoes
★ 2 tablespoons tomato paste
★ 1 teaspoon dried oregano
★ 1 teaspoon sugar
★ $^1/_2$ teaspoon salt
★ freshly ground black pepper

Heat the oil in a saucepan, add the onion and garlic, and cook over medium heat for 5 minutes. Stir in the chopped tomatoes, tomato paste, oregano, sugar, salt, and black pepper. Bring to the boil. Lower the heat and simmer for about 15 minutes, stirring from time to time. Serve with pasta.

Spaghetti

Serves 4–6

You will need:

★ 2 tablespoons oil
★ 1 onion, finely chopped
★ 1 garlic clove
★ 1 lb. (450g) lean ground beef
★ 1 lb. (450g) tomatoes, fresh or canned
★ beef stock cube
★ 1 teaspoon dried basil
★ 1 bay leaf
★ $^1/_2$ teaspoon salt
★ freshly ground black pepper
★ $1^1/_4$ cups (300ml) water
★ grated Parmesan cheese, to serve

Heat the oil in a saucepan, add the onion and garlic, and cook over medium heat for 5 minutes. Brown the meat, stirring constantly. Add the chopped tomatoes, basil, bay leaf, salt, pepper, and water, and sprinkle in the stock cube. Bring to the boil, reduce the heat to low, cover, and simmer for 20 minutes. Remove the bay leaf and serve with grated Parmesan cheese.

Variations

Other easy pasta toppings include any of the following:
☆ olive oil and chopped fresh basil leaves
☆ butter
☆ any grated cheese
☆ pesto
☆ tuna fish
☆ chopped fresh tomatoes

Instead of beef, you can use ground turkey and a chicken stock cube.

B-B-Q news

It's fun eating outdoors, and the great advantage is that it doesn't matter if any of the children drop their food or make a mess!

Mini chicken satay

Makes 8–10 skewers
You will need:
★ 3 boneless chicken breasts
For the marinade:
★ 4 tablespoons soy sauce
★ 1 teaspoon sesame oil
★ 1 tablespoon honey
★ 1 tablespoon sherry or rice wine
For the satay sauce:
★ 6 tablespoons peanut butter
★ 1 clove garlic, crushed
★ 1 tablespoon soy sauce
★ ¹/₂ teaspoon chili oil
★ 4 tablespoons water
★ 1 tablespoon rice, or wine, vinegar
★ wooden skewers, soaked in water
   to prevent them from burning

Cut the chicken into ¹/₂-inch (1cm) cubes and thread about 10 onto each skewer. Make the marinade by combining all the ingredients. Pour over the skewered chicken and set aside for 1 hour. Barbecue the chicken for about 10 minutes, turning frequently. Meanwhile, make the satay sauce. Put all the ingredients into a food processor and blend until smooth. Serve the chicken skewers with the sauce.

Branded potatoes

Brand spuds with the initials of the guests or the age of the birthday child. Draw on your design with the point of a small knife, then carve out the skin and bake the potato in the oven or wrapped in foil in the coals.

B-B-Q tips

☆ **Make sure the barbecue grill is very hot before you start to cook.**
☆ **Brush the grill or griddle with a little oil to prevent the food from sticking.**
☆ **Keep cooked meat well away from raw meat to avoid contamination.**

Cut the corn cobs into pieces to make them easier to eat.

Corn on the cob

You will need:
- ★ I ear of corn per person
- ★ butter, to serve
- ★ salt and pepper

Husk the corn, making sure to remove all the silky threads. Dip it into cold water then wrap it tightly in aluminum foil. Grill on the barbecue, turning it frequently, for about 10 minutes. Serve with lots of butter, salt, and pepper.

Mini-burgers

Makes about 18 burgers
You will need:
- ★ Ilb. (450g) ground beef
- ★ salt and pepper
- ★ 18 mini-buns
- ★ lettuce leaves, to serve

Lightly season the meat and form it into small, round, meatball-sized balls. Then flatten them into patties. Cook them for about 3 minutes each side on the griddle (they will be too small for most grills). Serve in the mini-buns with a few lettuce leaves, and offer a selection of relishes for the children to help themselves.

Arrange all the barbecued food on a big platter and allow people to help themselves.

Vegetable kebabs

Makes 6–8 kebabs
You will need:
- ★ 8 cherry tomatoes
- ★ 12 mushrooms
- ★ 2 zucchini, sliced
- ★ I red bell pepper, cubed
- ★ I onion, cut into quarters
- ★ 6–8 wooden skewers

For the barbecue sauce:
- ★ 4 tablespoons ketchup
- ★ 2 tablespoons Worcestershire sauce
- ★ I 1/2 tablespoons honey
- ★ I teaspoon lemon juice
- ★ pinch of cayenne pepper

Mix all the barbecue sauce ingredients in a saucepan, and cook over a low heat for about 5 minutes, stirring constantly. Remove from the heat and cool. Thread the vegetables onto the skewers, alternating the colors. Brush with the sauce, and grill on the barbecue for 10 minutes.

Barbecue tools
- ☆ Spray bottle of water (to put out burning fat)
- ☆ Tongs and spatula for turning
- ☆ Dish towel for wiping hands
- ☆ Platter for cooked food

Sweet endings

No kids' party is complete without lots of treats. Satisfy even the strongest sweet tooth with these fun recipes.

Meringue mini-beasts

Makes about 15 mini-beasts
You will need:
- ★ 4 egg whites
- ★ 1 cup (250g) fine
- granulated sugar
- ★ food coloring
- ★ candies, to decorate

Heat the oven to 250°F (130°C). Line baking sheets with nonstick baking paper. Beat the egg whites until stiff. Add the sugar and continue beating for about 10 minutes. Divide the mixture into bowls and add a few drops of coloring to each one. Pipe each color separately onto the baking sheets in shapes that could include ladybugs, caterpillars, spiders, mice, and snails. Decorate with candies. Bake for 2 hours, then leave to cool.

Coconut squares

Makes 10-12 squares
You will need:
- ★ 2 cups (450g) fine granulated sugar
- ★ $5/8$ (150ml) milk
- ★ $1 2/3$ cups (150g) shredded coconut
- ★ pink food coloring

Line a 8-inch (20cm) square cake pan with foil. Dissolve the sugar in milk over low heat. Bring to the boil and simmer for 10 minutes. Remove from heat and stir in the coconut. Pour half the mixture into the pan. Color the other half pink and pour quickly over the first layer. Leave until slightly set, then mark into equal squares, refrigerate, and cut or break when cold.

Cookie faces

Makes 20 cookies
You will need:
★ 20 large sugar cookies
★ glaze icing
★ food coloring
★ selection of candies, to decorate

Spread the icing on the cookies. Leave the icing to set for a few minutes, then add the candy decorations.

Chocolate apples

Makes 4 apples
You will need:
★ 6 oz. bittersweet chocolate chips
★ 4 popsicle sticks
★ 4 apples
★ sprinkles, to decorate

Melt bittersweet chocolate chips in a heatproof bowl in the microwave for about 3–5 minutes on high power. Alternatively, you can melt over a pan of simmering water, then remove from the heat. Push the popsicle sticks into the apples, then dip into the melted chocolate. Leave to harden slightly on foil, then decorate with sprinkles.

Brownies

Makes 12 brownies
You will need:
★ 6 oz. (170g) dark chocolate
★ ¹/₂ cup (115g) unsalted butter
★ ¹/₂ tablespoon baking powder
★ ¹/₂ cup (55g) unsweetened cocoa
★ 4 large eggs, separated
★ 1¹/₄ cups (300g) fine granulated sugar
★ ¹/₂ teaspoon almond extract
★ 1 teaspoon vanilla extract
★ 1¹/₂ cups (170g) all-purpose flour, sifted

Preheat the oven to 375°F (190°C). Line a 9 x 11-inch (23 x 28cm) baking pan with waxed paper. Melt the chocolate, butter, and cocoa in a heatproof bowl in the microwave on high power for 1¹/₂ minutes, or over a pan of simmering water. Set aside to cool slightly. Beat the eggs and add the sugar and the almond and vanilla extract. Gently stir in the cooled chocolate mixture, and add the flour, a little at a time. Pour the mixture into the pan and bake in the center of the oven for 20–25 minutes. The outside should be firm and the inside slightly gooey. Remove from the oven and cool before cutting into portions. Dust with confectioner's sugar before serving.

Chocolate cookie popsicles

Makes 15 popsicles
You will need:
- ★ 1 cup (230g) butter
- ★ ¹/₄ cup (55g) fine granulated sugar
- ★ 1 egg
- ★ 1 cup (115g) chocolate malted powder, dissolved in 2 oz. (55ml) hot milk and cooled
- ★ 3 cups (340g) all-purpose flour
- ★ ³/₄ cup (85g) cake flour
- ★ 4 oz. (115g) dark chocolate, grated
- ★ 6 oz. (170g) each milk and dark chocolate, melted
- ★ sprinkles and candies
- ★ 15 popsicle sticks

Heat oven to 350°F (180°C). Line two baking sheets with waxed paper. Beat the butter, sugar, and egg in a bowl till light and fluffy. Stir in the chocolate malted mixture, gradually add the flour and grated chocolate, then chill. Put the mixture on a lightly floured surface, and roll until about ¹/₂ inch (1cm) thick. Cut into shapes resembling fruit pops about 1¹/₂ x 3¹/₄ inches (4 x 8cm) and ¹/₂ inch (1cm) thick. Transfer to baking sheets and insert the popsicle sticks. Bake for 15 minutes, or until lightly colored. Leave to cool for 5 minutes before transferring to a cooling rack. Dip into melted milk or dark chocolate and decorate with sprinkles and candies before the chocolate sets completely.

Fruit pops

Makes 4 fruit pops
You will need:
- ★ 2 tubs of fruit yogurt, such as strawberry and banana, or plain yogurt with sugar to taste
- ★ small pieces of fruit of your choice
- ★ 4 popsicle molds

Push the popsicle sticks into the molds. Mix the yogurt with your chosen fruit and spoon the mixture into the molds. Level the tops with a knife. Put the molds in the freezer. Remove when the pops are set, about 2–3 hours later. Dip the bottom of the molds in hot water to make it easier to loosen the frozen fruit pops.

Decorate your chocolate popsicles with sprinkles and candies.

Ginger shapes

Makes about 45 ginger shapes
You will need:
* ★ 1 tablespoon oil
* ★ 3 cups (340g) all-purpose flour
* ★ 1 teaspoon (5ml) baking soda
* ★ 2 teaspoons (10ml) ground ginger
* ★ ½ cup (115g) unsalted butter, cubed
* ★ 1 cup (170g) brown sugar
* ★ 1 egg
* ★ 4 tablespoons corn syrup
* ★ selection of candies
* ★ glaze frosting
* ★ ribbon

Heat oven to 350°F (180°C), and oil 3 baking sheets. Mix flour, baking soda, and ginger in a mixing bowl. Add the butter and mix in with fingers until mixture resembles fine breadcrumbs. Add the sugar. Mix the egg and corn syrup in a separate bowl. Pour it into the flour mixture, and stir until it forms a dough. Turn out on a floured surface and knead for 5 minutes. Roll out until about ½ inch (1cm) thick, cut into shapes, and put on the baking sheets. Bake for 15–20 minutes. Allow to cool slightly, cut a hole for the ribbon with a tiny piping tube, and transfer to a rack to cool. Decorate with glaze icing and candies, and leave to set. Thread ribbon through the holes and hang them up.

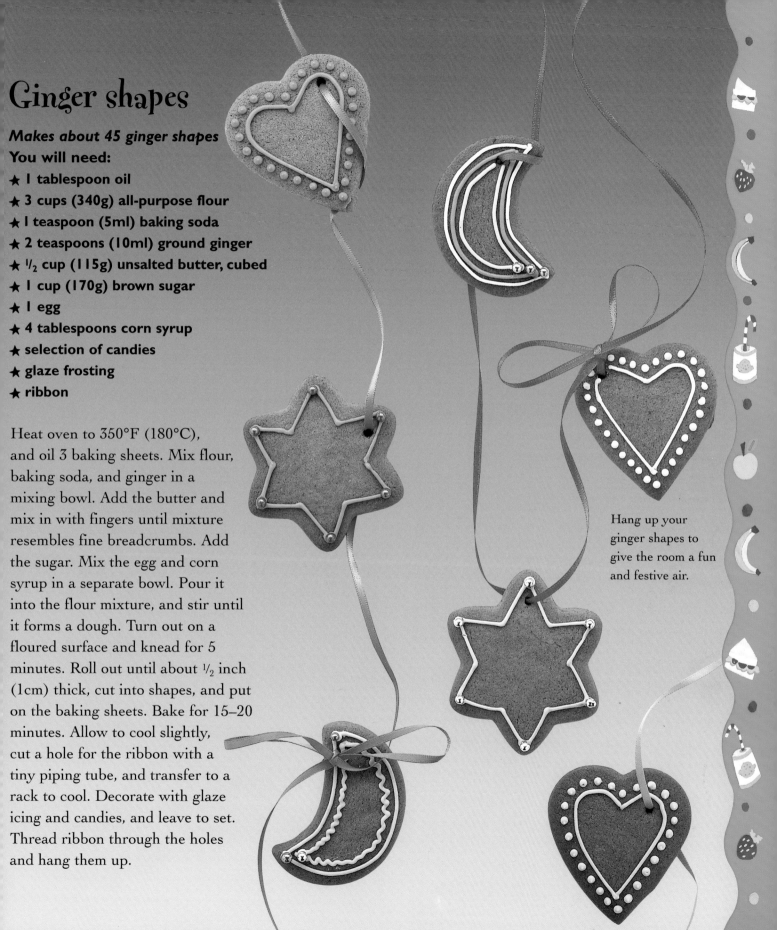

Hang up your ginger shapes to give the room a fun and festive air.

Kids' cocktail time

Parties are thirsty work. Quench the children's thirst with these delicious drinks.

Hot chocolate

Makes 1 large mug
You will need:

★ **2 tablespoons unsweetened cocoa**
★ **3 tablespoons boiling water**
★ **2 teaspoons sugar**
★ **1 cup (240ml) hot milk**
★ **marshmallows, to decorate**

Dissolve the cocoa in the boiling water. Then stir in the sugar and the hot milk. Finally, top the hot chocolate with a few marshmallows.

Hot chocolate is a favorite in cold weather.

Royal lemonade

Makes 6 glasses
You will need:

★ **juice of 6 fresh lemons**
★ **1lb. (450g) ripe strawberries**
★ **10 tablespoons sugar**
★ **3 pints (1.4 liters) water**

Put the fruit and sugar in a blender, and whizz up. Pour into a pitcher and add water.

Royal lemonade looks as good as it tastes.

Ice cream soda

Makes 2 glasses
You will need:

★ **1¼ cup (300ml) 7-Up**
★ **1 sliced banana, 1 sliced kiwi fruit**
★ **4 scoops vanilla ice cream**

Set aside a few slices of fruit. Put the rest of the ingredients into a blender and whizz until frothy. Pour into a tall glass and decorate with fruit or a colorful swizzle stick.

You can also make ice cream soda with cola.

Slurpies

Makes 4 glasses
You will need:

★ 12 oz. (350ml) orange juice
★ 12 oz. (350ml) pineapple juice
★ 12 oz. (350ml) cranberry juice

Freeze the juice in separate ice trays. Store the frozen cubes in plastic bags. Blend the ice cubes into a slush. Arrange colored layers of ice in tall, tapered glasses.

Slurpies are great for hot summer days.

Banana shake

Makes 4 milkshakes
You will need:

★ 1¼ cups (300ml) pint milk
★ 6 tablespoons heavy cream
★ 8 scoops vanilla ice cream
★ 2 bananas, sliced
★ 5 drops vanilla extract
★ cocoa powder and chocolate sprinkles, to decorate

Put all the ingredients, apart from cocoa powder and sprinkles, into a blender, and whizz up till thick. Pour into chilled glasses and decorate.

Shakes are easy to make.

Fruit punch

Makes 1 glass
You will need:

★ ¾ cup (175ml) 7-Up
★ ½ cup (120ml) mixed tropical fruit juice
★ 2 tablespoons grenadine syrup
★ 1 slice of pineapple
★ 1 maraschino cherry
★ 1 toothpick

Half-fill a glass with 7-Up. Tip the glass and carefully pour the fruit juice down the side. Repeat with the grenadine syrup. Serve with a pineapple slice and a cherry speared on a toothpick.

Use any combination of fruit juices and fruit to make an exotic cocktail.

Making cocktails special

☆ Serve in pretty glasses, available in different shapes and sizes.
☆ Use plastic glasses to prevent accidents.
☆ Decorate with swizzle sticks and toothpicks.
☆ Serve with straws, which come in a range of styles and colors.
☆ Be generous with ice.

Basic cake & cookie recipes

Sponge cake

You will need:

★ 1 1/4 cup (280g) butter or margarine

★ 1 1/4 cup (280g) fine granulated sugar

★ 5 medium-size eggs

★ 1 1/4 cup (280g) sifted cake flour

Preheat the oven to 350°F (180°C). Grease two 8-inch (20cm) round cake pans. Cream the butter and sugar together in a mixing bowl until light and fluffy. Beat in the eggs, one at a time, then slowly add the sifted flour. Pour the mixture into the prepared pans and bake for 35–40 minutes, or until the surface of the cake springs back when pressed. Leave to cool in the cake pan for 5 minutes, then turn out onto a cooling rack.

Flavorings

☆ **Chocolate:** dissolve 2 tablespoons of unsweetened cocoa powder in 2 tablespoons of hot water, adding after the flour.

☆ **Lemon:** add the grated rind of a lemon and 1 tablespoon of lemon juice.

Pound cake

You will need:
- ★ ³/₄ cup (170g) butter
- ★ ³/₄ cup (170g) sugar
- ★ 3 eggs
- ★ 2 cups (230g) sifted cake flour
- ★ 2 tablespoons milk

Preheat the oven to 325°F (160°C) and grease a bread pan, at least 9 x 5 x 3 inches (23 x 13 x 8cm) in size. Cream the butter and sugar together in a bowl until light and fluffy. Beat in the eggs, one at a time, adding a little flour. Fold in the rest of the flour. Add enough milk to form a dropping consistency. Pour the mixture into the prepared pan and bake for 1–1¼ hours, or until the cake springs back when pressed. Remove the cake from the oven, and allow it to cool for 5 minutes. Then turn the cake out onto a cooling rack and allow it to cool completely.

A recipe for roll-out fondant icing:

¹/₂ oz. gelatin ★ ¹/₄ cup water ★ ¹/₂ cup corn syrup ★ ³/₄ oz. glycerine ★ 2 lbs. icing sugar

Dissolve the gelatin in water and heat over hot water bath. Put sugar in large bowl and add gelatin, corn syrup, and glycerine. Mix until smooth. Adjust consistency with water or sugar. Wrap until used.

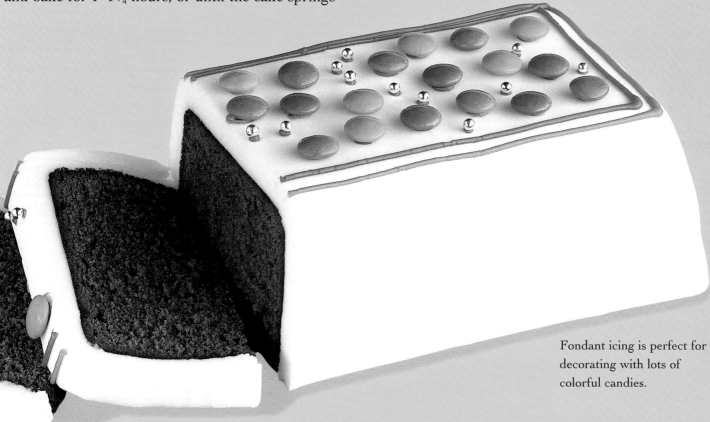

Fondant icing is perfect for decorating with lots of colorful candies.

Carrot cake

You will need:

★ 1 cup (115g) all-purpose flour
★ 1 teaspoon cinnamon
★ pinch of grated nutmeg
★ $1/2$ teaspoon salt
★ $1^2/_3$ cups (300g) soft brown sugar
★ 8 fl oz (250ml) vegetable oil
★ 3 large eggs, beaten
★ 3 cups (270g) grated carrots
★ $1^1/_2$ cups (170g) chopped walnuts (optional)
★ butter for greasing the cake pan

Preheat the oven to 350°F (180°C). Grease and line a 10-inch (25cm) round, deep cake pan. Sift the flour, spices, and salt into a large bowl. Mix the sugar and oil in another bowl, then add the eggs. Make a well in the flour, stir in the liquid, then add the carrots and the walnuts, if using. Spoon the mixture into the pan and bake for $1–1^1/_4$ hours, or until a skewer inserted into the cake comes out clean. Allow to cool in the pan, then turn out on a cooling rack.

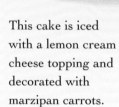

This cake is iced with a lemon cream cheese topping and decorated with marzipan carrots.

A nutty choice

Try using almonds instead of walnuts. But always make sure that no one is allergic to nuts.

Butter cream

You will need:

★ $1/4$ cup (50g) unsalted butter
★ 1 cup (115g) sifted confectioners' sugar

Cream the butter and confectioners' sugar together in a bowl. Butter cream can be used either between layers of cake or on top of the cake, as preferred.

Glaze frosting

You will need:

★ 2 cups (230g) sifted confectioners' sugar
★ 3–4 tablespoons hot water

Put the sugar in a bowl, and pour on the hot water, mixing as you go, until the frosting leaves a ribbon trail on itself when the spoon is lifted.

Lemon topping

You will need:

★ 1 cup (230g) cream cheese
★ grated rind of $1/2$ lemon
★ $1/4$ cup (30g) confectioners' sugar

Mix the cream cheese and lemon rind together, and stir in the sugar. Spoon the mixture over cake, and smooth it over with a spatula.

Sugar cookies

You will need:

- ★ ¹/₂ cup (115g) unsalted butter, plus a little extra to grease the cookie sheets
- ★ ¹/₂ cup (115g) fine granulated sugar
- ★ 1 ¹/₂ cups (170g) all-purpose flour, plus a little extra for rolling out
- ★ 1 egg, beaten
- ★ pinch of salt
- ★ 1 teaspoon vanilla extract

Preheat the oven to 350°F (180°C). Beat the butter and sugar together until light and fluffy. Sift the flour into the bowl. Add the egg, salt, and vanilla extract, and mix well. Knead the dough for a few minutes until it forms a ball. To make cookies, break off 12 small pieces of dough and roll each one into a ball. Place the balls, well-spaced, on a greased cookie sheet and flatten each one a little with your fingertips. Bake the cookies for 12–15 minutes or until a light golden brown.

Flavorings

To make chocolate chip cookies, add 4oz. (125g) of chocolate chips along with the vanilla extract.

Gingerbread

You will need:

- ★ 3 cups (340g) all-purpose flour
- ★ 1 teaspoon baking soda
- ★ 1 tablespoon ground ginger
- ★ ¹/₂ cup (115g) butter
- ★ 1 cup (170g) soft brown sugar
- ★ 1 egg
- ★ 4 tablespoons corn syrup

Preheat oven to 350°F (180°C). Mix the flour, baking soda, and ginger in a bowl. Mix in butter till mixture resembles fine bread crumbs. Beat egg and syrup together in a separate bowl, then add to flour mixture and mix until it forms a ball. Knead on a floured work surface. Refrigerate for 1 hour. Roll out to required thickness and cut into shapes. Bake for 10–15 minutes according to size.

Novelty cakes

Butterfly cake

You will need:

★ 1 sponge cake, made with 4 eggs, 2 cups (230g) all-purpose flour, 1 cup (230g) fine granulated sugar, and 1 cup (230g) butter, baked in a 9-inch (23cm) round cake pan
★ butter cream frosting, made using 1 cup (230g) butter and 3 cups (450g) confectioners' sugar
★ pink, blue, yellow, and green food coloring
★ 1 large chocolate log
★ a selection of candies
★ 2 birthday candles with holders

Cut the cake in half, and make cuts into the sides to form wings, as shown. Place the chocolate log in between the two wings to form the butterfly's body. Make the butter cream frosting and divide into 4 separate bowls for the different colors. Color most of the frosting pink, and the rest blue, yellow, and green. Cover the cake with pink frosting. Spread yellow, blue, and green frosting on top of the pink frosting and mix together, forming a rainbow pattern. Decorate with candies and arrange candle holders and candles at the top of the cake to form antennae.

Volcano cake

You will need:

★ 2 chocolate cakes— 1 baked in an oven-proof mixing bowl, capacity 1 quart (1 liter) and 1 in a smaller bowl, using a basic pound cake recipe
★ chocolate butter cream frosting
★ orange glaze frosting
★ a selection of candies
★ sparklers (optional)

Place the smaller cake on top of the larger cake, and cut to form a volcano shape. Hollow out a crater. Cover the cake with chocolate butter cream frosting and a few candies to look like molten lava. Add the orange glaze frosting to form the flow of lava. Stick in a few red, orange, and yellow candies to look like molten boulders.

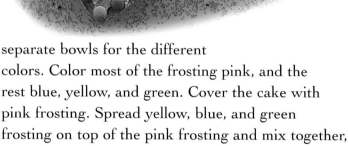

For a touch of drama, light three sparklers in the volcano's crater.

Rocket cake

You will need:
- ★ 4 large chocolate-coated chocolate logs
- ★ 1/2 cup chocolate butter cream frosting
- ★ 2 mini chocolate logs
- ★ 6 fan wafers
- ★ 8 oz. (250g) melted chocolate
- ★ colored balls, sprinkles, and red hots, to decorate
- ★ 1 ice-cream cone

Stand 3 chocolate logs together on a cake board and secure them with chocolate butter cream frosting. Place the fourth log on top of the others and again secure with frosting, then arrange the mini chocolate logs around the bottom, as shown. Dip the edges of the fan wafers into the melted chocolate, then stick colored balls on the edges. Place the wafers around the rocket as shown. Dip the ice-cream cone in melted chocolate, roll the cone in sprinkles, and place upside down on top of the rocket. Stick on candies to decorate.

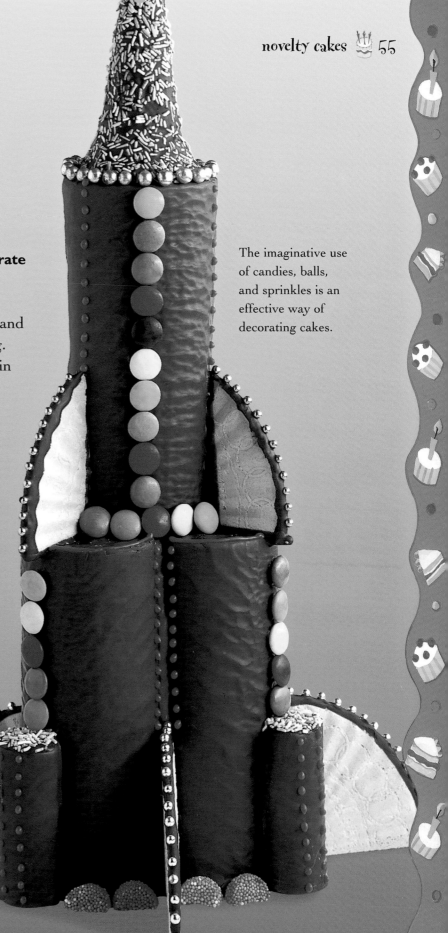

The imaginative use of candies, balls, and sprinkles is an effective way of decorating cakes.

Assembly

You don't have to be an accomplished cakemaker to produce some very impressive novelty cakes. Simply assembling ready-made cakes, such as chocolate logs, and decorating them with melted chocolate, frosting, and candies can be just as effective.

Princess castle cake

You will need:

★ **2 large chocolate logs, cut in half horizontally to make the four towers**

★ **1–1½ cups (250–350g) butter cream frosting**

★ **3 square sponge cakes, 6 x 2 inches**

★ **(15 x 5cm) deep**

★ **4 ice-cream cones**

★ **8 petits fours, cut in half**

★ **a selection of candies, silver balls, gumdrops, and sprinkles, to decorate**

Cover each chocolate log in pink butter cream frosting. Cut a small triangle from each corner. Cover the cones with frosting and then roll them in the sprinkles. Leave to set. Decorate the castle with petits-fours, ice-cream cone towers, and candies, securing them all with butter cream frosting.

A fragile cake like this is best assembled on a board where it will remain throughout the party.

A door made from wafer cookies and a sidewalk and windows made from gumdrops are nice finishing touches.

Treasure chest cake

You will need:
- ★ 1 chocolate pound cake made in a 9 inch (23cm) bread tin
- ★ chocolate butter
- cream frosting
- ★ yellow marzipan (or almond paste)
- ★ a selection of candies

Cut the top third off the cake to form the lid. Gouge a hollow inside the chest. Spread the insides with chocolate frosting, and fill the chest with candies—preferably ones that look like jewels. Reassemble the cake. Cover the outside with chocolate frosting, and smooth with a spatula dipped in hot water. Roll the marzipan into a long thin sheet and cut it into narrow strips. Lay them on the chest, pressing them gently into the frosting.

Angelfish cake

You will need:
- ★ 1 pound or sponge cake, flavored with the grated zest and juice of 1 lemon and a pinch of cinnamon, baked in a 9-inch (23cm) round cake pan
- ★ 3 x 8oz. (250g) roll-out fondant icing (see recipe on p. 51)
- ★ blue, green, and yellow food coloring
- ★ apricot jelly
- ★ a selection of candies, to decorate

Cut out cake shapes for the fish, as shown in the picture. Color the three blocks of fondant icing yellow, green, and blue. Brush the cake with warmed apricot jelly. Roll out the icing on a surface sprinkled with confectioners' sugar, one color at a time, and cover the body with yellow and blue stripes and the face, tail, and fins with the green frosting. Don't forget to carry the icing on over the sides of the cake. Decorate the fish with candies for the eyes and mouth, and little blobs of blue frosting to suggest bubbles.

Knead in enough food coloring, using clean rubber gloves, for the desired intensity.

Soccer cake

You will need:
- ★ I pound cake, baked
  in an oven-proof mixing bowl, capacity
  1¹/₄ pints (600ml), for 50 minutes
  at 350°F (180°C)
- ★ white roll-out fondant icing
- ★ blue food coloring
- ★ apricot jelly

Turn out the cake and trim to make a ball shape. Roll out half the white fondant icing and cut into hexagons. Color the remaining fondant icing blue, roll out, and cut into hexagons. Brush the cake with a thin layer of apricot jelly and, starting with a blue hexagon at the top, arrange the hexagons on the cake. If you like, you can outline the definition between hexagons with an icing pen, as shown.

To remove ice cream from pan, soak a dish towel in hot water, wring out, and wrap around pan.

You must work fast because the ice cream melts quickly.

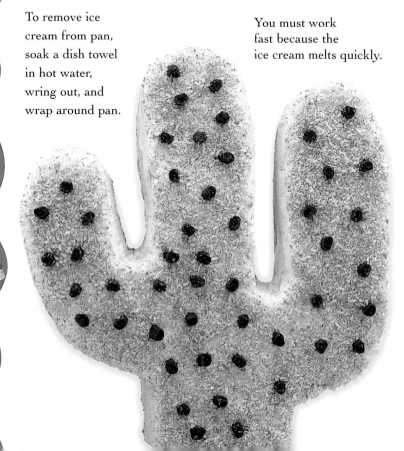

Cactus cake

You will need:
- ★ 3 quarts (3 liters) ice cream
- ★ mint chocolate sticks
- ★ shredded coconut
- ★ green food coloring,
  for coconut

Spoon the ice cream into a 9-inch (23cm) round spring-form cake pan. Smooth with a spatula. Return to the freezer till solid. Meanwhile, cut out a cardboard template of a cactus. Take the ice cream out of the freezer and remove it from the pan. Cut out the cactus shape quickly, and put the cut-out shape back in the freezer till solid. Remove from freezer, push chocolate sticks into the ice cream to resemble cactus spikes, and sprinkle with green shredded coconut. Return to the freezer until you are ready to serve.

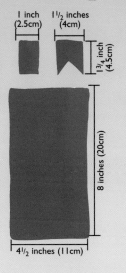

Farmhouse cake

You will need:

★ 3 quantities gingerbread dough
★ 1 cup (300g) glaze frosting
★ butter cream frosting
★ food coloring
★ candies, for decoration

Make cardboard templates and cut out the shapes for the farmhouse. Heat the oven to 350°F (180°C). Roll out the gingerbread and cut to the desired shapes. Transfer to a cookie sheet lined with waxed paper. Bake in the top of the oven in batches for 12–15 minutes. Place on a wire rack to cool. Cut out animal shapes, put in oven and bake for 7–10 minutes. Remove and cool on a wire rack. Stick the farmhouse together with frosting, starting with the walls, then adding the roof and the chimney. Decorate the animal shapes with frosting in different colors. Assemble the farmyard scene on a board covered in green butter cream frosting.

Farmhouse cake templates

A wisp of cotton ball smoke coming out of the chimney gives the farmhouse a cozy air.

Cookie clown

You will need:
★ I quantity of chocolate chip cookie dough
★ I quantity of white glaze frosting
★ colored, roll-out fondant icing
★ candies

Heat the oven to 350°F (180°C). Roll the cookie dough into a large circle about 1¼ -inch (3cm) deep, using a plate as a guide. Transfer it to a greased cookie sheet and bake for 20 minutes. Transfer the cookie to a cooling rack.

Cover the cookie with a thick layer of glaze frosting.

Making faces

This cookie is decorated with a clown's face, but you could also make a cat, a rabbit, or even someone you know!

Make a mouth and nose using colored fondant icing and decorate with candies.

Numbers

Celebrate a birthday in style with a special cake made in the shape of the birthday child's age. This is surprisingly easy to do. Just use one or two pound cakes in the shapes and sizes detailed here...

You will need:
2 loaf cakes, each 10 x 3½ inches (25 x 8cm)

You will need:
I rectangular cake, 11 x 7 inches (10 x 3½ inches) (25 x 8cm) (28 x 18cm); I loaf cake

You will need:
2 ring cakes, each 8 inches (20cm)

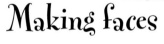

You will need:
I rectangular cake, 11 x 7 inches (28 x 18cm)

Polly parrot

You will need:
- ★ I quantity of plain cookie dough
- ★ pale and dark green glaze frosting
- ★ M&Ms and jelly beans

Preheat the oven to 350°F (180°C). Roll out the cookie dough into a rectangle about 12 x 6 inches (30 x 15cm). Lay the dough on a cookie sheet, and bake for 25 minutes. Cool slightly, and then, using a template, cut parrot and branch shapes from the dough. Use the scraps to make some leaves.

When the cookie is cool, spread the pale green glaze frosting. Then, using the picture as a guide, decorate the parrot with candies.

Other shapes

We've made a cookie parrot—and he looks splendid—but there is no reason why you can't make any other shapes that you like— such as a cat, a train, or a boat. Simply choose any of your child's favorite things and make your own template.

Cover the branches and leaves with dark green glaze frosting.

You will need:
I loaf cake, 10 x 3½ inches (25 x 8cm); I ring cake, 8 inches (20cm)

You will need:
I loaf cake, 10 x 3½ inches (25 x 8cm); I ring cake, 8 inches (20cm)

You will need:
2 loaf cakes, 10 x 3½ inches (25 x 8cm)

You will need:
I large ring cake, 8 inches (20cm); I small ring cake, 6 inches (15cm)

You will need:
I loaf cake, 10 x 3½ inches (25 x 8cm); I ring cake, 8 inches (20cm)

You will need:
I loaf cake, 10 x 3½ inches (25 x 8cm); I ring cake, 8 inches (20cm)

Breaking the ice

The first half-hour of any party can be awkward. Some children may not know anyone, and some may be shy. Children will arrive at slightly different times, which can be difficult for a newcomer.

The name game

Before the party, write out the names of each guest on a piece of stiff paper. Color the letters and cut out each one. Prepare another strip of stiff paper with a piece of adhesive-backed Velcro attached to the back. Finally, make a chart of all the children's names, and pin this to the wall—just in case they don't know how to spell their names. Scatter the letters through-out the room, and as the children arrive, ask them to hunt for the letters of their name. Once they have found them, ask them to stick them onto the piece of stiff paper with adhesive-backed Velcro on the back to make their own name badge.

Hunting for stars

You will need a pack of little stars. The tiny thumbnail size are the best ones to use. Hide them around the room before the party begins, keeping in mind that they should be within the children's reach and that should depend on the children's age. The idea is that the children collect as many pairs—two stars of the same color—as they can, and the person who finds the most wins.

Color a hat

Cut out hat shapes and put them on the table along with crayons or markers for the kids to color in. The hats can be themed to match the party, or just simple ones that the children can decorate as they like.

Silly hats help break the ice.

Rogues' gallery

You may need a helper with this game, depending on the age of the children, as those who are younger will probably need some assistance. Prepare a craft table, with lots of paper, crayons, and markers, and ask the children to draw a self-portrait. As they finish the drawing, ask them to write their name on the back and pin it up on the wall, or on a board. Each one wins a prize.

Where's the honey pot?

Paint a large picture of a woodland scene. On the back, draw a honey pot, and check that this is visible from the front when you hold the picture up to the light. Write each child's name on a teddy bear card, and tell the children to position the teddy bear where they think the honey pot is hidden, using double-sided tape. When each child has had a turn, hold the picture up to the light to see whose teddy bear is closest.

The yarn trail

Tie a candy bar to different-colored balls of yarn—one for each of the guests. Hide the candy bars and gently unravel the yarn around the room, trying not to tangle the different colors. Lay a more or less complicated route according to the age of the guests. As they arrive, give each child a piece of yarn to match their ball, and ask them to start searching.

A hat can make a child feel special.

Variations on a theme

Other things to draw could be a dinosaur, a cat, or a car, depending on their age and their interests.

It's difficult to be in a bad mood when you're wearing a funny hat.

Children love dressing up in hats from a very early age.

Noisy games

There's nothing quite like a good noisy game for letting off steam. As long as you can stand the noise, here are a few suggestions for having a lot of fun.

Fish in the sea

This is a good chasing game for a confined space. Sit the children down in a circle, facing inward. Choose the names of three fish, and walk around the circle, naming the children in sequence—cod, mackerel, and shark, cod, mackerel, and shark, and so on. You then have several of each fish sitting at intervals. Explain that when their name is called, the fish have to get up and go for a swim. This entails walking clockwise around the outside of the circle and listening to what happens. Talk them through the game: when you say the sea is rough, they run; when you say it's getting rougher, they run faster; when you say the tide turns, they turn and run in the other direction; and when you shout "STORM," they have to run back to their original spaces. The last to arrive is out and has to sit in the circle facing outward.

Musical cushions

For this game, you need a cassette player and a cushion or pillow for each child playing. Scatter the cushions on the floor. While the music plays, the players walk or dance around the room. Once it stops, each child must sit on a cushion with no part of their body touching the floor. At the start of each new round, one cushion is removed. The player who finds him or herself stranded without a cushion once the music stops is out. The last player left wins the game.

Musical dressing up

Make a collection of clothes that the children can put on. Decorate four boxes, each one with a different color. Put one in each corner of the room and fill it with some clothes in the same color as the box. Play music for the children to dance to. When the music stops, they have to run to whichever color you call and put on something from the box. When all the clothes have been used up, hold a fashion show to see what everyone looks like.

Flying saucers

The players all dance around in a circle to lively music. When the leader calls, "Flying saucers sit down in twos" (or threes or fours...), everyone rushes to get into a group of the number called. Those who are last to sit down or who are left out of a group are out. The last two left in the game are the winners.

Crossing the river

Stretch a length of drawer-lining paper or wallpaper across the center of the room. This represents the river that the children have to run across while you play music. Anyone who is in the river when the music stops is considered to have "drowned." The winner is the last one to be left "alive."

On the stroke of midnight

This game requires plenty of space. The children dance to music until you clang a saucepan lid loudly to announce the approach of midnight. At this point, all the children rush to a given spot, or through an open door, or leap onto the sofa—whatever you have told them they should do. The last child to do this is out. Repeat the music and "chimes" until only one child is left—who is the winner.

Spiders and flies

This is a very active game, which children really enjoy. One person is "it," or the spider. He or she rushes around yelling, "I need some flies for my web," and tries to catch as many children—who run around being the flies—as possible. Once a fly has been caught, he or she has to stand still, with legs apart, until released by one of the other flies who hasn't been caught. To do this, he or she has to crawl between the legs of the child who is the fly caught in the web. This can go on for a long time, so put a time limit on it to let other children have a turn being the spider.

Quiet games

There are moments at almost every party when the children become overexcited after playing noisy games. This is the time to calm them down by playing some quiet games such as these.

Pass-the-parcel

Although this game has music, it is an excellent one for calming children down when they have been very active. Choose as many little prizes, such as candies or markers, as there are guests, plus one larger one for the main prize. Wrap all the prizes in several layers of newspaper or old wrapping paper, beginning with the main prize. The children sit in a circle and pass the parcel around to each other. When the music stops, they have to unwrap as many layers as possible in order to win a prize before the music starts again. When playing this game with young children, watch what is happening carefully and try to make sure that every child wins a prize.

"Pass-the-parcel" is a a lot of fun for children of all ages.

Memory game

This can be as simple or as difficult as you like, depending on the age of the children. To take part in this, the children must be able to write reasonably well. Arrange some toys on a tray, and cover them with a cloth. Give each child a piece of paper and a pencil. Remove the cloth and give the children 60 seconds to memorize as many of the items as possible. They then have to write down as many of the items as they can. The child who remembers the most items correctly is the winner.

Variations on a theme

Show the children a tray of goodies for 60 seconds. Then remove some of the items and ask them to write down what's missing.

Statues

Choose one player to be the statue master. The master stands with a prize next to him or her, and back to the other players. The players must sneak up on the master while his or her back is turned. When the master turns around to look—which can can be done as often as the master likes—the players must freeze into "statues." If the master sees a "statue" moving, that person is out. The winner is the first person to reach the prize without the master seeing him or her move.

Variations on a theme

This game can be adapted for other parties. The statue master can be a witch for the Spooky party; an alien for the Space party; or a sheriff for the Wild West party.

Sleeping lions

Choose someone to be "it." The children lie down and become sleeping lions. They lie flat on their backs, keeping as still as possible—there's absolutely no giggling allowed! The "it" person has to try to make them laugh by making funny faces but not actually touching them. Anyone who giggles is out. The last lion left in is the winner.

Variations on a theme

This game can easily be adapted to fit any of the themed parties—for example, Sleeping clowns, Sleeping astronauts, Sleeping pirates, Sleeping cowboys, or whatever appeals to your child most.

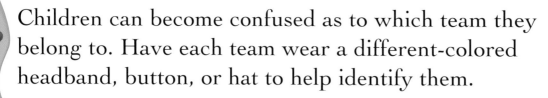

Team games

Children can become confused as to which team they belong to. Have each team wear a different-colored headband, button, or hat to help identify them.

Flopping fish

This is a team relay race. Cut a fish shape from tissue paper for each team. The children must fan their fish along the ground with a newspaper from one line to another. The first one over the finish line wins. The children then flop their fish around a chair and back to their team for the next player's turn.

Boat race

Divide the children into teams of about six. They sit in a line with their legs wide apart and with their arms around the waist of the person in front. When you say "go," all the crew must shuffle their bottoms to move themselves forward, but the line cannot be broken or the team has to start again. The winning team is the first to cross the finish line.

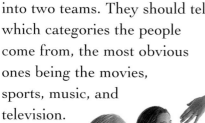

Who am I ?

This game is similar to charades, but the children have to mime a famous person. Divide the children into two teams. They should tell which categories the people come from, the most obvious ones being the movies, sports, music, and television.

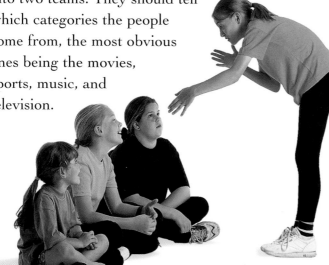

Flounder on the line

This team relay race can be played in a relatively confined space, wherever you can hang two clothes lines. Put ten clothes pins on each line. Stand the team in a starting position as far away as possible. The first child in each team runs to the line, unclips the clothes pins (the flounder) as fast as possible, and runs and hands them to the second child, who runs and puts them back onto the line again (the bait), and so on until everyone has had their turn. To make it more difficult for older children, you can penalize them for dropping any clothes pins by removing these from the game. The winning team is the one that has caught the most flounder.

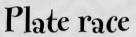

Plate race

Mark out a river, about 6½ feet (2m) wide, across the center of the room. Divide each team so that half the members are sitting on either side of the river. The first child in each team holds two paper plates and when you say "go," they have to cross the river using the plates as stepping stones. They put down the first plate and step on it, then put the next plate ahead while standing on one foot and step onto that one, then lift the back foot and move the original plate forward and so on (not as easy as it sounds!). When they reach the other side, they hand the plates to the first person in the line, who crosses back again.

Googly balloons move around the room in a very silly way.

Googly balloons

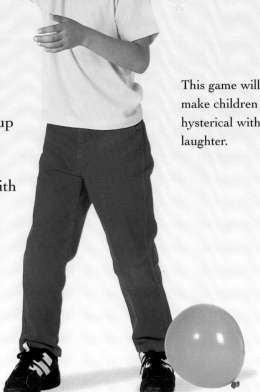

Blow up balloons, putting a small marble through the neck of each one before you tie the end. This weighs the balloons and makes them move in unexpected ways. Release into the group one more balloon than children. The object is to keep the balloons up in the air. Play this in two teams, each side with an extra balloon. The team who lets a balloon drop to the floor first loses.

This game will make children hysterical with laughter.

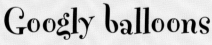

Outdoor games & activities

When the children need to run around and let off steam, plan an outside activity party, either in the backyard or in a park. But remember—it would be unwise to feed them before all that boisterous exercise!

Crab race

You need plenty of room for this race—a large lawn is ideal. Line up the children in a row and show them how to hold their ankles and run like a crab. Arrange a finish line no more than 11 yards (10m) away. Any child who lets go of his or her ankles or falls over is automatically out of the race. The winner is the first child over the line.

3-legged race

The children pair off with a partner, and tie their center legs together with a scarf. Then they have to run the race with "three legs." Pairs of a similar height and build tend to be the best, though the sight of a one-small-and-one-large pair can be very funny.

Wheelbarrow race

This is another race that is run in pairs. One person stands in front of the other. The person in front puts his or her hands on the ground, while the person in back lifts the legs of the person in front. Then they run the race in this position.

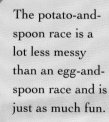

The potato-and-spoon race is a lot less messy than an egg-and-spoon race and is just as much fun.

potato-and-spoon race

This is a variation on the egg-and-spoon race. The children have to run an allotted distance carrying a small potato balanced on a spoon. If the potato falls off the spoon, the child must pick it up without his or her fingers touching the potato and start all over again.

Balancing a potato on a spoon requires concentration.

Sack race

Each competitor climbs into a large sack and races by jumping along with their feet in the sack. Any large bag will do, but plastic garbage bags are ideal. Make sure no one puts his or her head in the bag.

Obstacle course

Plan an obstacle course, including fun things like crawling under a blanket, hopping over large stuffed animals, skipping ten times, doing a somersault, and so on. If you are in a large yard, you may be able to try more adventurous things like swinging on a rope from a tree. Include about six to ten activities, and show the children what they have to do before they begin.

Bobbing for corks

Corks are a good alternative to apples, which are often too big for little mouths. This is a very wet game that is best played outside. Put a bowl, half-full of water, on the ground and place several corks in it. Tell the children to get the corks without using their hands— and keep a towel handy for drying off wet faces!

Flowerpot race

Each of the competitors has a pair of flowerpots. When the "go" is given, they each step onto one of them and put the other pot in front, without allowing the free foot to touch the ground. They then step onto the front flowerpot and balance on this one, reaching back to lift the pot behind and put that one in front. Anyone who loses their balance and falls over has to start all over again.

Games for the very young

Below are some suggestions for games that are perfect for very young children. All the games require supervision by an adult, who can direct the proceedings and make sure that no one cheats!

Tommy

This is a very simple game but never fails to delight children. You need a dish of M&Ms. One person is "it" and has to leave the room, while the others choose a color to be Tommy. The child returns and eats an M&M out of the dish. If no one says anything, he or she takes another color, and another, until he or she takes the color that is Tommy, at which point all the children yell and someone else is chosen to be "it."

Cats and dogs

Before the party begins, scatter a selection of brightly-colored buttons around the house and, if the weather is good, the backyard. Divide the children into two teams—the cats and the dogs. Each team has an adult leader. The object of the game is to find all the buttons.

When each one is found, the cats meow to call their leader, and the dogs bark to call theirs, because only the leaders can pick them up. The team that has the most buttons at the end of the game wins, and each team member should be given a prize.

Oink!

First of all, the player who is "it" is given a small cushion and then blindfolded. All the other children sit in a circle on the floor. The child who is "it" is turned around three times and then has to find a player, put the cushion on their lap, and sit on it. He or she calls out, "Oink, Piggy, Oink," and the person underneath must oink very loudly. If the person who is "it" can name the oinker, they then swap places. If not, they have to find someone else to sit on until they can identify the oink. Whenever someone new takes over as "it," the other players all have to change places in the circle, after the blindfold has been put on.

What's the time, Mr. Wolf?

This is a game of chase. The wolf is the chaser, and the children are his prey. There is a safe place—a sofa or space in the room. The children follow the wolf around the room calling out, "What's the time, Mr. Wolf?" If he replies with any time such as "one o'clock," they are safe. But as soon as he calls out "dinnertime," they have to run for safety. Anyone who is caught takes the place of Mr. Wolf.

In and out of the bluebells

The children stand in a circle with a space between each one of them and an adult as the leader. They all sing this song together:

In and out the dusty bluebells
In and out the dusty bluebells
In and out the dusty bluebells
Who will be my partner?

Tippy tippy tap tap on my shoulder
Tippy tippy tap tap on my shoulder
Tippy tippy tap tap on my shoulder
You will be my partner.

The leader taps a child on the shoulder, and that child puts his or her hands on the leader's shoulder or waist (depending on height). The two of them weave in and out of the circle, singing the song, and choose another child. And so on until all the children are joined together.

Lost teddy bear

Stand the children in a large circle facing inward—all except for one child who is holding a teddy bear in his or her arms. This child now walks outside the circle in a counterclockwise direction and drops the teddy bear behind another child of his or her choice. The second child picks up the teddy bear and races the first child around the circle to sit in the empty space. The child who is left standing then walks outside the circle in a counterclockwise direction and drops the teddy bear behind another child of his or her choice—and the next round begins. The game continues in this way until all the children have had their turn.

Perfect party favors

Every child who's invited to a party nowadays expects to go home with party favors. Selecting all the party favors is therefore an essential part of organizing the party.

Party favors can add a tremendous additional expense to what is already a very costly event. But with a little bit of imagination, you can cut the cost considerably and still give the children something really special to take home with them.

Homemade party favors

There are many things that you can make for the children's party favors. What you make depends on whether your skills lie in the cookery or the crafts field. Ideas include:

★ cookies
★ candies
★ toffee apples
★ coin purses
★ key rings
★ buttons
★ handmade jewelry
★ masks
★ decorated baseball caps

Can I help?

Kids love making party favors for their friends to take home.

Buying party favors

Toy stores, party stores, stationery stores, even supermarkets—they all offer a wide range of things you can buy for party favors. To keep it from getting too expensive, set yourself a limit—say, $1.00 or $2.00 per child. That may sound too difficult but you'll be surprised at how inexpensive party favors can be.

★ pens, pencils, crayons
★ mini candy bars
★ stickers
★ playing cards and dice
★ books and notebooks
★ soap and shower gel
★ bags of candy
★ personalized balloons
★ bead kits
★ face paints
★ hair ornaments
★ jewelry

★ badges
★ coloring books
★ pencil sharpeners
★ erasers
★ packs of raisins
★ bubbles
★ shells
★ fold-up fans

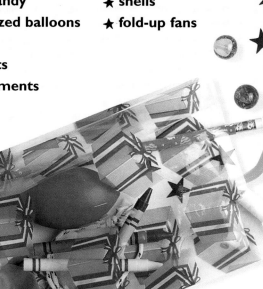

Traditionally, the piñata is brightly colored and made in the shape of a donkey.

Mexican piñata

How the party favors are presented is important, and something slightly different will add to the excitement.

In Mexico, the piñata is a traditional party decoration. It is made out of newspaper and is filled with candies and small gifts. The traditional piñata is made in the shape of a donkey, but you can make one in any shape you like, according to the theme of the party—a fish, a flower, a fairy, an animal, or whatever your child would like. It is hung up as a decoration throughout the party and then, when the rest of the games are over, the children hit it with a stick until it breaks open and all the candies and presents fall out.

For many kids, a major part of the fun are the party favors that they're given before they go home.

Making a piñata

You will need:

- ★ I large balloon
- ★ plaster of paris
- ★ scraps of newspaper
- ★ poster paints
- ★ colorful tissue paper, crepe paper streamers,
- or cellophane
- ★ craft knife
- ★ twine or thin rope
- ★ selection of candies and little presents

1 Blow up a large balloon and tie the neck in a double knot.

2 Cover the balloon with a layer of newspaper strips. To do this, first wet the strips of newspaper one at a time, and then layer onto the balloon until it is completely covered in newspaper strips and is itself invisible.

3 Repeat the whole process until the balloon has at least three layers of newspaper around it. Allow the plaster of paris to dry thoroughly—this will take as long as one or two days, depending on how many layers of newspaper and plaster you have applied.

4 Paint the piñata with poster paint in bright colors. Decorate with crepe paper streamers, tissue paper, or cellophane.

5 When the piñata is completely dry, cut a small opening in the top of it. Pop the balloon. Make a couple of holes with the knife on each side of the opening, and thread the twine or rope through it for hanging up. Finally, fill the hole with a selection of candies and little presents.

Countdown

There always seems to be so much to do and never enough time to do it in. Organization is the answer. Keep a countdown to the big day handy, and avoid any last-minute panic. Good luck!

4 weeks to go...

★ Select party theme and venue.
★ Decide on the number of guests and make a list.
★ Choose your helpers.
★ Make and send the invitations.
★ Book the entertainer, if you are having one.

3 weeks to go...

★ Organize transportation to and from the venue.
★ Make the piñata (see page 75), and any homemade party favors.

2 weeks to go...

★ Buy or make any decorations or props.
★ Buy paper plates and cups, napkins, balloons, and candles.
★ Make the costumes.
★ Plan the games and make a list.
★ Choose the music.

1 week to go...

★ Buy non-perishable ingredients for the food.
★ Buy any ready-made party favors and prizes.

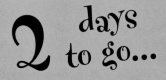

3 days to go...

★ Baking day: bake the cookies and birthday cake.
★ Choose party clothes, and wash and iron them.

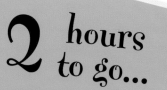

2 days to go...

★ Make any food that needs to go into the freezer.

1 day to go...

★ Decorate the house and table.
★ Prepare the first aid kit.
★ Buy all the perishable items of food.
★ Wrap up party favors.
★ Fill the piñata.
★ Wrap prizes for games.

8 hours to go...

★ Prepare the games.

2 hours to go...

★ Make the fresh food and drink.
★ Blow up the balloons.
★ Put a sign and balloons on the mailbox or front door to show guests where the party is.

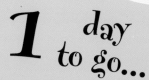

1 hour to go...

★ Set the table.
★ Put the food out.

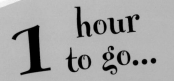

Your problems solved

Above all, parties should be fun—but they're not without their problems. We have the answers to some of the most common ones.

My daughter is six and her whole class at school is usually invited to parties. I just don't have the space.

You could take all the children out —to an inexpensive restaurant, say, for a pizza or hamburgers. Or just tell your daughter that you do not have the room and that she can invite just six of her best friends. She won't get as many presents, but you won't have as much hassle.

I can't afford the birthday present my child has his heart set on. What can I do?

Tell him the truth. Parties and birthdays are expensive occasions. One solution might be to say that you can afford to buy half of it and maybe he can contribute the other half through savings and odd jobs. Or you could ask all the relatives to contribute to one big, extra-special gift.

My older daughter is jealous that her younger sister is having a party. How do I help her overcome these feelings?

A good way to deal with this problem is to include your older daughter in the preparations for the party and ask her to organize some of the games. She'll feel a lot better if she feels involved.

My son wants his dad (my ex-husband) at his birthday party. We have hardly spoken since the divorce, and I really don't want him there. Am I being unfair?

It is important for your child to have a relationship with his father. Make sure that his father knows all the details—when, where, etc. Next, stress that it would be better if he came on his own. And finally, find out exactly when he is arriving so your son won't be disappointed. There's nothing wrong with putting an ending time on it, too—after all, the other guests have been given one.

I do not get along with my mother-in-law. She is so bossy and insensitive, but I feel it is important for her to be part of all our family celebrations. What should I do?

The best way to deal with this situation is to involve your mother-in-law in some way. Ask her to help with the food for the adults, say, or to be in charge of taking children to the bathroom.

I do not have time to make party favors for the children who are coming to the party. What can I buy for them instead, and how much will I need to spend?

There are plenty of options for you to choose from. You should expect to spend at least $1.00 to $2.00 on each child. For this amount you can buy a decent toy, or a selection of pencils, beads, or shells. When you buy in bulk, you can ask for a discount. You can also include a few miniature candy bars.

First aid

With so many children running around, minor accidents can happen. Keep a list of contact telephone numbers handy in case of an emergency. Below is a quick reference guide for dealing with partytime mishaps.

Bruises: Raise the bruised area and apply a cold compress in the form of an ice pack or frozen peas.

Dry burns and scalds: Immerse the injury in cold water for ten minutes. Remove any constrictive clothing, and apply a dry, sterile dressing.

Fainting: Lay the child down, with legs raised, and make sure the airway is clear by loosening any clothes around the neck, chest, and waist. Check for injury.

Foreign bodies in the eye: If the foreign body is embedded, seek medical help. If there is dust or an eyelash in the eye, seat the child in a chair facing the light. Stand behind the child, with his or her head resting against you. Separate the eyelids with your index finger and thumb and flood the eye with water (preferably sterile), using an eyecup to wash out the foreign body. Or lift it out with the corner of a clean, damp cloth.

Grazes: Clean the area under running water. Protect the wound with a sterile dressing while you clean the surrounding area, then cover with a Band-Aid.

Stings: For a sting in the mouth, give the child ice cubes to suck and seek help. For a sting elsewhere, remove it with tweezers and apply a cold compress.

Nosebleeds: Seat the child with his or her head leaning forward. Pinch the nostrils for at least ten minutes, holding a bowl under the nose to catch any blood. If bleeding persists, repeat at ten-minute intervals. Once the bleeding has stopped, do not allow the child to blow his or her nose.

Splinters: Clean the area with soap and water. Sterilize some tweezers in a flame and gently pull out the splinter along its entry line.

Sprains: Immobilize the area, then apply a cold compress in the form of an ice pack or frozen peas. Apply a pad of cotton, secured with a bandage, and keep the limb raised until the pain subsides.

Vomiting: Offer reassurance, wipe the child's face with a cool, damp cloth, and encourage him or her to rest quietly in a cool room, with a bowl close by in case vomiting occurs again. Offer small sips of water.

Have on hand: sterile dressings, bandages, and water ★ eyecup ★ Band-Aids ★ tweezers ★ absorbent cotton ★ ice packs or bags of frozen peas.

Index

Acknowledgments

We would like to thank Heidi Tibbles, 34 Ridge Street, Watford, Hertfordshire (01923 254609) for making the children's costumes, and Stephanie Spyrakis, Creative Faces, 52a Sutton Road, London N10 1HE (0181 444 4489) for painting their faces. We would like to thank Party Party, 11 Southampton Road, London NW5 4JS (0171 267 9084) for lending us props, and Charles Bradley for making some of them. Thank you, too, to Rachel Fuller, for helping us out in the office, and Paul Supplee of Byerly's Minnesota, for cake advice. And last but not least, we would like to say a particularly big thank you to all the following children for having their pictures taken: Anastasia Barker; Miriam Blume; Becky Greber; Emily Greber; Thomas Gage; Lucy Johnson; Adam Lofthouse; Lisa Milner; Yasmin Milner; Peter Milsom; James Moller; Samuel Oladeinde; Lucy Rands; Dan Richmond; Hannah Scott; Alistair Tweedale; and Edmond Wood.